VERULAMIUM

The Roman City of St Albans

Rosalind Niblett

TEMPUS

First published 2001

PUBLISHED IN THE UNITED KINGDOM BY:

Tempus Publishing Ltd
The Mill, Brimscombe Port
Stroud, Gloucestershire GL5 2QG

PUBLISHED IN THE UNITED STATES OF AMERICA BY:

Arcadia Publishing Inc.
A division of Tempus Publishing Inc.
2 Cumberland Street
Charleston, SC 29401
1-888-313-2665

Tempus books are available in France, Germany and Belgium
from the following addresses:

Tempus Publishing Group	Tempus Publishing Group	Tempus Publishing Group
21 Avenue de la République	Gustav-Adolf-Straße 3	Place de L'Alma 4/5
37300 Joué-lès-Tours	99084 Erfurt	1200 Brussels
FRANCE	GERMANY	BELGIUM

British Library Cataloguing in Publication Data.
A catalogue record for this book is available from the British Library.

ISBN 0 7524 1915 3

Typesetting and origination by Tempus Publishing.
PRINTED AND BOUND IN GREAT BRITAIN

Contents

List of illustrations

Text figures

Colour plates

Acknowledgements

The enormous debt owed to previous excavators of Verulamium, in particular to Sir Mortimer Wheeler and Professor Sheppard Frere, will be immediately obvious to anyone reading this book. In addition however it is a pleasure to be able to acknowledge the help and support of the large number of friends and colleagues who have helped me to write it. The encouragement and help provided by present and former members of the staff of the Verulamium Museum, and by members of the St Albans and Hertfordshire Architectural and Archaeological Society, has been invaluable. I must also thank especially Chris Saunders, Adrian Havercroft, Simon West, Stuart Bryant, Clare Halpin and staff of the Hertfordshire Archaeological Trust for discussing the results of their work, and supplying information often in advance of their own publications. Any suspect interpretations of their findings presented here, however, are of course my responsibility, not theirs. Acknowledgements and thanks are also due to the British Museum for permission to reproduce **colour plates 3** and **20**, and to the Society of Antiquaries of London for permission to reproduce figure **2**. I am also grateful to Sheppard Frere for figures **11**, **13**, **33** and **68**, and **colour plates 10** and **21**, to Charles Dobson for taking colour photographs including **colour plate 1**, and to Roger Preston for flying the aircraft. Except where otherwise indicated, the other photographs are reproduced by permission of the St Albans Museums Service, whose copyright they are, and I owe an especial debt to Jennifer Golding, the museum photographer and image librarian, for her advice, expertise and above all her patience and good humour in the face of my many requests for help. I am glad to be able to thank publicly Philip Dean, Terry Hunn, Alex Thorne and David Williams whose line drawings appear here, and who invariably managed to transform my often scruffy plans or sketches into first-class drawings. Finally particular thanks are due to my long-suffering husband Robert who has undertaken the Latin translations and has, as always, remained a tower of strength.

1 Abbots, antiquarians and archaeologists
1000 years of archaeological enquiry

> (Abbot Ulsinus) loved the district and people of St Albans and looked after their interests. He brought the people from the surrounding area together and made them live in the town itself, providing and enlarging a market place. He helped them construct buildings by providing money and materials. He built the churches of St Peter to the north, St Stephen to the south and St Michael to the west . . . [1]

This brief reference to the foundation of a 'new town' on the site of modern St Albans, on the north side of the river Ver, close to the Abbey of St Alban, was recorded over three centuries later by the historian monk, Matthew Paris. It marks the final depopulation of Roman Verulamium, once one of the largest and most prosperous towns of Roman Britain. With the loss of nearly all its inhabitants, the abbey authorities of the day were not slow to realise the value of the abandoned town as a convenient source of building material. The late tenth and early eleventh centuries were a time when extensive rebuilding was being planned, both for the Abbey church and the monastery. There was a need for a large supply of building material, the remedy was conveniently to hand, and the systematic destruction of Verulamium commenced.

Nevertheless, the same monks who were responsible for so much destruction in the Roman town were also the first to record details of the buildings they were demolishing. Here again Matthew Paris is the source:

> Abbot Ealdred (*c*.980), having examined ancient writings found underground, from the old city of Verulamium, pulled down and filled in everything. He knocked down, filled in and blocked up the rough places and streets, together with the underground passages, which had been solidly and skilfully built with arches, some of which formed the underground water system which had once flowed round much of the city . . . When the diggers were doing this, they found next to the river bank some oak planks with nails in them, soaked in shipbuilding pitch, as used on the hulls of boats. They also found some naval equipment, such as anchors half eaten by rust, and oars made of fir-wood, which provided definite proof that the waters of the sea had once carried vessels to Verulamium . . .

Further discoveries were made under Ealdred's successor:

> . . . Abbot Eadmar (*c.*AD 1000) carefully searched through the depths of the earth where the remains of the city of Verulamium appeared. He found and kept aside ancient stone slabs, with tiles and columns which he needed for the fabric of the church which he intended to build for St Alban. In the foundations of the old buildings and in the underground hollows the diggers found urns and amphorae, well made of clay on the potter's wheel, and also glass jars, containing the ashes of the dead . . . Above these were found half-ruined temples, overturned altars and statues . . . [2]

Paris was writing in the first half of the fourteenth century but must have had access to much earlier accounts, preserved in the monastery. We can assume that as early as the tenth century St Albans monks were sufficiently interested in Verulamium to produce what could be claimed to be the earliest excavation report in the country.

No doubt an important reason for this monastic interest in the town's Roman past was related to an entry in the *Historia Ecclesiastica Gentis Anglorum* written by the Northumbrian monk, Bede, in the early eighth century. Bede clearly states that the early Christian martyr, Alban, was not only an inhabitant of Verulamium but that he was put to death just outside the town, and buried there. Seventy years after Bede's death Offa, king of the Mercians, had extended his kingdom to include St Albans. Once firmly established here Offa turned his attention to Alban himself. Bones were discovered and triumphantly identified as those of the martyr, and a monastery was established on the supposed site of the martyrdom itself. It was the planned enlargement of this late Saxon monastery in the tenth century that led to the demolition of so much of the former Roman town (**colour plates 1** & **2**).

The monastery, and with it the cult of St Alban, flourished throughout the Middle Ages. This alone would have ensured that the town's Roman past was never forgotten. In addition to this however, the election in 1249 of a local man, Nicholas Breakspear, as Pope Adrian IV led to St Albans acquiring the status of the premier abbey in England. This status, and a succession of able and scholarly abbots, secured for the abbey a place in the forefront of artistic, religious and intellectual centres. Evidence of its importance is recorded in the *Gesta Abbatum Sancti Albani*, an account of the history of the abbey from the traditional date of its foundation in 793-1401. It was the work of various writers, including the chronicler Matthew Paris (who died in 1259) and Thomas Walsingham (abbot during the reign of Richard II), and is liberally peppered with references to the Roman town.

In the later sixteenth century the Reformation not only saw the almost total destruction of the monastic buildings but also the suppression of the cult of St Alban. By now however, there was a growing interest in the classical world, and Verulamium continued to catch the interest of scholars and writers. Furthermore, because medieval St Albans had grown up, not on the same site as the Roman town, but on the supposed site of the martyrdom of Alban approximately a kilometre to the north-east, traces of Roman Verulamium were still clearly visible, rather than being buried beneath later buildings

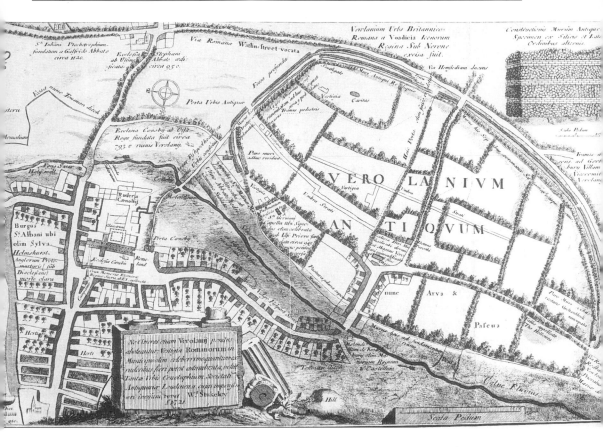

1   William Stukeley's map of Verulamium in 1722. Photograph St Albans Museum Service

(**colour plate 1**). The 'King's Antiquary', John Leland, recorded the robbing of a length of Watling Street in 1531, and noted 'pipes — made of baked tiles, but rounded, of which each was inserted into the end of the other — I also saw a place now encumbered with fruit trees, where, it is with all probability conjectured, was the palatium of Verulamium'. Slightly later William Camden included a brief description of Verulamium in his *Britannia,* remarking that 'nothing of it now remains but ruins of walls, chequered pavements and Roman Coins now and then digg'd up'. One of the earliest historical accounts of St Albans was written in 1631 by a local man, John Shrimpton.[3] Shrimpton was interested not only in the Roman town, but also in the history of St Albans as a whole. He recorded details passed down by word of mouth on the religious practices in the monastery and the daily life of the monks, as well as personal recollections of traces he had found as a boy of the second battle of St Albans in 1461. Like Camden's however, his account of Verulamium was taken almost entirely from written sources, notably Tacitus and Bede.

The early eighteenth-century antiquary William Stukeley made a number of visits to the town. Stukeley was keenly interested in all aspects of the town's past and seems to have spent his time energetically recording any visible remains, both in the Roman town and in the precinct of the former monastery. In 1721 he published an 'ichonography' of Verulamium[4] showing the position of the various 'vestigia' of which he knew (**1**). He returned the following year while compiling his *Itinerarium Curiosum*, published in 1724. In the course of a somewhat rambling account, he remarked that:

> . . . Infinite are the antiquities of all sorts that have been, and frequently are, dug up at Verolam. When I was making an ichonography of it, I could have taken several pecks of remainders of Mosaic pavements out of a little ditch near St Germans chapel; and there is one or two intire yet under ground. As you walk along the great road that runs north and south through the city from St Michaels Church, you see foundations of houses and streets, gutters, floors, etc under the hedge-rows . . .

Destruction of both Roman walls and streets was, however, clearly still rampant. In previous visits Stukeley had observed the lines of streets showing up as parched bands in the ripening crop but in 1724 he noted, with obvious disapproval, that they were being constantly used as quarries to provide road metalling, observing that

> . . . three years ago a good part of the wall was standing; but ever since, out of wretched ignorance, even of their own interest, they have been pulling it up all around, to the very foundations, to mend the highway; and I met hundreds of cart-loads of Roman bricks, etc., carrying for that purpose as I now rode through the old city . . .

Although he left no further notes on Verulamium, Stukeley continued to make occasional visits to St Albans, as he is referred to in notes made by a local antiquarian, Joshua Webster. Webster was a doctor, practising in the town in the 1740s and '50s. He was clearly a man with many interests and talents, with a wide circle of friends, including the artist William Hogarth. Webster was in the habit of making notes on anything of interest that came his way. These were brought together in a notebook, now preserved in the library of the Society of Antiquaries. Whether Webster ever intended to publish his records more widely is not known, but his methods and motives for making the compilation are perhaps best summed up in his own words:

> The author of the following brief account of the ancient City of Verolam and St Albans, having liv'd there some years, had consequently opportunities of observing many circumstances relating to the antiquities of both places, that appeared to him remarkable; fill'd up part of his leisure time, in collecting such remains as he cou'd procure, being chiefly solicitous of obtaining what information he cou'd find from the vestiges of a long since demolished City, now turn'd into Farm and Corn field, and such an information as might be both usefull and amusing; tho' it may not immediately point out any certainty in the Historical events, yet will convey to the reader a tolerable Idea of the Taste and Genius of those remote times. In this light the writer of the following

2 *Joshua Webster's sketch c.1745 of the Folly Lane/Oysterfield area. The size of the ditches surrounding the hill has almost certainly been exaggerated.* Reproduced courtesy of the Society of Antiquaries of London

sheets may be view'd as a Gleaner in a Cornfield, willing to pick up every Grain he cou'd find, good bad or indifferent, and in such shapes he presents them in the following pages . . .

Webster's notebook is indeed something of a hotchpotch. Between 1740 and 1765 a host of items caught his interest ranging from 'curiously shaped stones' and Roman and medieval antiquities to geology and natural history; a description of a bee orchid is slotted between a list of Saxon abbots and a sketch of a lump of pudding stone with no attempt to link the three. He was obviously a keen amateur artist and he illustrated his notebook with watercolour sketches many of which one suspects he 'improved' or 'embroidered' (**2**). Naturally Webster reflects the spirit of his own time. Like all educated men of the period, he was well versed in the classics, but he was also heavily influenced by the beginnings of the Romantic movement. His description of the Oysterfield hill, north of Verulamium is typical. He explains the site's unusual name as deriving from that of an early governor of Roman Britain Ostorius Scapula; in fact the name probably derives from the Old English *eoweste* (Eastern).

Stukeley and Webster are only two of what appears to have been a group of largely local antiquaries, interested in the town's Roman past, who made sporadic records of chance discoveries throughout the eighteenth and early nineteenth centuries. In 1780 Richard Gough referred to burials being discovered, apparently in the area now known to be a late Roman cemetery west of Branch Road. Further burials in this same cemetery were made in 1799 and 1813. In 1799 a local antiquary, James Brown, recorded the discovery in this area of an inhumation burial in a lead coffin, while in 1813 a burial in a stone coffin and accompanied by fine glass vessels was uncovered at Kingsbury, close to Back Lane, the old road to Redbourn.[5] Written records however are sporadic, and most record chance finds of isolated burials. Stukeley and his pronouncements clearly influenced views of Verulamium for at least a century after his last recorded visit here in 1746. In that year Webster recorded the discovery of a mosaic floor; he included a sketch of it in his notebook, but the floor itself was immediately broken up by the '. . . concourse of people gathered . . . in hopes of finding hidden Treasure underneath it'. Webster does not tell us precisely where in Verulamium the floor was found, but he added that Dr Stukeley (who saw it) 'supposed it to be the floor of a court of Justice'. Whether this was the same building as Leland's *palatium*, we shall never know. A century later another local man, John Harris, drew up a plan of Verulamium showing the site of the Forum as identified by Stukeley. This is placed in insula XI immediately south-east of the actual site of the Forum/Basilica complex. No nineteenth-century excavations are known in this *insula*, but it seems likely that this is the site of the 1746 discovery, and Stukeley's Basilica, or 'Court of Justice'. Presumably this specific identification of the Basilica site was either recorded in some now lost source, or was simply received wisdom among the group of local antiquaries, informal forerunners of the modern St Albans and Hertfordshire Architectural and Archaeological Society.

As the nineteenth century progressed, there was a steady increase in written accounts and records. Summaries of St Albans' past were published in 1808 and 1815.[6] These included accounts of Verulamium based largely on Camden and Stukeley, but both added a few more recent discoveries, including a brief reference to items kept in the Watching Loft in St Albans Abbey, overlooking the shrine of St Alban. For much of the nineteenth century however, local antiquarian interest was focused on the Abbey, which at the time was in imminent danger of collapse. However, with men like John Evans, Richard Grove Lowe and Thomas Wright all active in the area, there was little chance that earlier remains would be ignored. In 1845 growing interest in the town's past led to the formation of the St Albans Architectural Society, a title expanded later to the St Albans and Hertfordshire Architectural and Archaeological Society. This society, the 'Arch and Arch' as it is commonly referred to today, was to have a lasting and profound influence on the development of archaeology in St Albans in the years ahead.

One of the first sites with which the new society was faced was the Verulamium theatre. The identification of the theatre was the result of a chance observation in 1847 by a local engineer, Richard Grove Lowe, and his *'Description of the Roman theatre at Verulam'* (1848) was the first paper that the new Society published. An article on the discovery in the Illustrated London News captures the enthusiasm and optimism that clearly surrounded the work:

> . . . The Earl of Verulam with great kindness and good feeling has permitted a full exploration to be made; and it is to be hoped that every assistance will be rendered to the St Albans Architectural Society in their laudable exertions in investigating a site so pregnant with valuable remains. Mr Smith stated that he believed the entire plan of the ancient city might be discovered, with the foundations of most of the buildings, public and private . . .

A contemporary sketch by F.W. Fairholt (**3**) shows the entire *cavea* excavated. How much more was excavated at this time is unclear, but the work also uncovered part of a massive masonry building on the opposite side of Watling Street (later shown to be part of the *macellum*).

REMAINS OF THE ROMAN THEATRE AT VERULAM.

3   A sketch by F.W. Fairholt of the excavations in the theatre at Verulamium in 1849, looking towards the east. St Albans Abbey Church and Cathedral can be seen in the left background and St Michael's church in the right background. Reproduced by kind permission of the St Albans Museum

The recognition of the Roman theatre and the increasing number of references in local papers and archaeological society transactions gradually established Verulamium as a important archaeological site. An early result of the growing appreciation of the place was its selection in 1869 by the British Archaeological Association as the venue for that year's summer meeting. Faced with the prospect of a large gathering of antiquarians and scholars spending the best part of a week examining the antiquities of the district, members of the 'Arch and Arch' apparently decided they were rather short of visible remains with which to impress their distinguished visitors. No doubt after considerable deliberation, it was decided to dig exploratory trenches across Verulamium in order to expose rather more. The result was a remarkable series of trenches dug close to the contemporary hedgerows (now largely vanished) and altogether totalling approximately 1.2km in length. Fortunately plans were drawn up by John Harris, which enable the position of the trenches to be estimated more or less accurately today (**4**). Less fortunately, the details of what was actually found in them are very sketchy. Flint and mortar foundations and a tessellated floor, presumably from a substantial town house, were uncovered in insula XXXV and several street surfaces were identified, allowing Harris to draw up a basic street

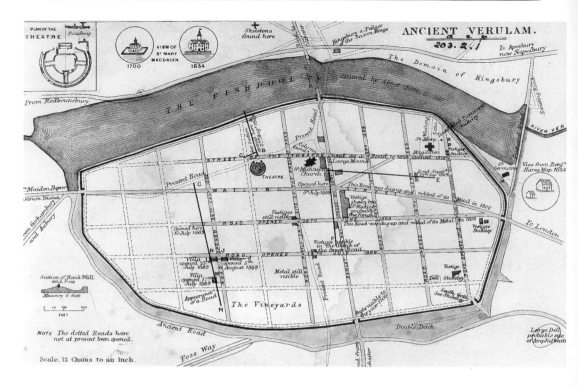

4   *John Harris' plan of the excavations at Verulamium in 1869.* Copyright St Albans Museum

grid for the whole town. The work also established the presence of the town wall along the north-west side of the town, but a tantalising reference to what were clearly the remains of burnt timber buildings is impossible to tie down to any particular area. In the event the afternoon devoted by the Association to visiting Verulamium was one of torrential rain, and the majority of the party curtailed their visit and sought the shelter of St Albans.

Whether there was further excavation on the theatre site at this time is not entirely clear. The idea was certainly mooted, and in reporting on her excavation of the theatre in 1935 Kathleen Kenyon noted that 'there seems to have been some excavation on the site in 1883 . . .'; however, she gives no source or further details. A further result of the Archaeological Association's 1869 visit was the publication by Grover of a paper devoted to the archaeology of the Roman town. This paper, *Verulam and Pompeii Compared* was published by the British Archaeological Association in 1869 and provides a useful summary of what was known about Verulamium in the mid-nineteenth century, as well as a fascinating insight into the attitudes of the mid-Victorians to the inhabitants of Roman Britain.[7]

It has to be admitted that as far as understanding of Roman Verulamium was concerned, Grover and his contemporaries did not know much more than what had been deduced by William Stukeley over a century before. Apart from the identification of the theatre and the discovery of a handful of burials which pinpointed two of the main cemetery areas of Verulamium, little was known of the town other than the basic layout of the streets and the approximate location of a few buildings with tessellated floors and flint and mortar footings. Just as Stukeley and Webster had reflected the romanticism of the mid-eighteenth century, so Grover and his contemporaries, working as they were when the British Empire was approaching its height, regarded Roman Britain from an entirely imperialistic and colonial viewpoint. This is admirably summed up by Grover, but was no doubt equally true of many, if not all of his contemporaries:

> Claudius, the Emperor of 'Reform Bill' celebrity, determined to add Britain to his unwieldy empire. He came, and saw, and conquered; and lo! Verulam is changed as by a magician's wand — a new city rises amidst the wigwams, and long straight streets of lordly mansions take the place of hovels. The princely frescoed villa rises where the hut stood. Then came temples to new gods; the forum, the *basilica*, and the law courts, filled with the *curiae*; knights, slaves, clients and a long array of imperial officials and tax-gatherers. . . . The grim centurion's voice tells of discipline and order and despotism, stern and unbending as of Prussia now. The droves of oxen and sheep for sacrifice approach the temples. Civilisation, with its blessings and curses, amazes the simple islander. A long cycle of magnificent imperialism for four hundred years has to be endured. It is the vestiges of this age which the spade reveals to us . . .

One feature of Harris' plans (4) that is immediately striking is the enormous lake shown lapping against the north and north-east walls of the Roman town. In 1869 Grove Lowe, perhaps influenced by a mental picture of the coastal towns in the Mediterranean, describes small boys fishing in the lake from the town walls of Verulamium. It is unlikely however that this was the only reason for the presence of the lake on his plans. In fact the idea that the entire valley floor up to the town walls was underwater arose long before Grove Lowe stumbled on the theatre. The valley was without doubt marshy, and probably subject to occasional flooding, but the existence of a lake, prior to the creation of monastic fishponds in the late Saxon period, rests ultimately on Matthew Paris' speculations on the origins of shells found by Abbot Ealdred's monks in the tenth century. The idea was taken up by Leland, Camden and Shrimpton, and gradually became accepted as fact. So persistent was the strength of this tradition, that it continued to influence archaeological thought well into the twentieth century.

Nineteenth-century concern about the state of St Albans Abbey led to attention being focused on the other medieval churches in the town as well. St Michael's Church, traditionally founded by Abbot Ulsinus in the tenth century, stands in the centre of Verulamium, and was the subject of a restoration programme by Gilbert Scott in 1865/6. In the course of this work massive foundations were observed under the tower; these foundations were recognised to be Roman, and from their size alone clearly belonged to a major public building. As a result archaeological attention was focused on the entire area around church and vicarage. Fortunately for archaeology, the vicar of St Michael's between 1895 and 1915 was Charles Bicknell, who was passionately interested in the

5 *Excavations in the garden of St Michael's Vicarage in c.1911.* Copyright St Albans Museum

Roman remains in his garden and in the adjoining glebe and churchyard. At the same time William Page was editing the Victoria County History and the two men obviously worked together on questions of Roman Verulamium. It might be expected that a late nineteenth-century vicar, with an interest in the Roman remains in his garden, would have had few qualms in uncovering sizeable areas. Charles Bicknell however had two problems. Firstly, either he or his wife was not prepared to sacrifice their carefully tended garden to unsightly excavations, and secondly the archaeological remains themselves were very deeply buried. The whole area lies in a shallow depression at the base of a steep slope. It seems likely that it had been terraced out of the base of the slope, probably in the early Roman period, and that subsequently large quantities of material had been washed downhill, burying the remains beneath up to 3m of overburden. Consequently the problems involved in excavating were (and still are) very considerable. In the garden itself, the demands of the garden meant that trenches could only be cut alongside paths, or where trees had to be replaced. Matters were somewhat easier in the vicarage glebe, on the south-west side of the garden. Here, although free from flower beds and fruit trees, the problem of depth was just as great, and indeed Mortimer Wheeler and Mrs Cotton, excavating here in 1949, were forced to abandon the project due to difficulties with the

6 *Tessa and Mortimer Wheeler sorting pottery at Verulamium in 1930.* Reproduced courtesy of the St Albans Museum, copyright reserved

depth of overburden. Nevertheless, between 1898 and 1911 Charles Bicknell and William Page excavated substantial areas (**5**). They identified the site of St Michael's Churchyard, vicarage and glebe as that of the Forum/Basilica complex, an identification that was confirmed some 50 years later by the discovery in 1955 of the Basilica inscription in the yard of St Michael's School. In Roman towns the Forum was an open space, usually surrounded by colonnades, where business was conducted. The Basilica was a large roofed building housing the law courts and administrative offices. Together the Forum and Basilica formed the business and commercial centre of the town.

Bicknell and Page excavated according to the standards of their time. Little dating evidence was recorded, although it is doubtful that much was found. Careful plans however were made; three phases of building were recorded and the results were published in the proceedings of the 'Arch and Arch' between 1899 and 1902. Thanks to the care exercised by the Society over the years, Page and Bicknell's original notes have been preserved and can still be consulted in the Society's archive. Using them it has been possible to rectify the one major misconception that Page and Bicknell's work gave rise to. The plan of the Forum/Basilica complex was published by Page in 1914 in volume 1 of the Victoria County History of Hertfordshire. This shows a large Forum, 103m wide and 81m long. This plan coloured most of the later accounts of the Roman town, implying as it did

17

that Verulamium had a large Forum, and that the street grid had been laid out before it was constructed. The 1914 plan, however, was not entirely accurate. The resulting misconceptions will be discussed in a later section (below p73-6); the important point here is that the achievement of Bicknell and Page was very significant. Their plan of the whole Forum/Basilica complex still presents problems, but their almost single-handed efforts are responsible for much of our knowledge of this, the largest building in Verulamium.

It was not until 1929 that the next landmark in the archaeology of Verulamium took place. In 1929 the City acquired what today is Verulamium Park, then fields covering approximately half the area enclosed by the Roman town walls. A condition of acquiring the land was that it should be used as a public park, but there also seems to have been a desire to lay out some of the Roman remains as a public attraction. With this in mind the mayor and corporation invited the young director of the Museum of London, Dr Mortimer Wheeler, and his wife Tessa Verney Wheeler, to undertake a programme of archaeological excavations here (**6** & **7**). Over the next four years the Wheelers directed a series of excavations which were to transform understanding of the Roman town, and to firmly establish Verulamium at the forefront of Romano-British studies.

Each summer from 1930-3 the Wheelers, with a large contingent of students, local volunteers and paid labourers, excavated an area that ultimately extended over 2.3ha in the southern part of the Roman town (**10**). The resulting excavation report, published in 1936 as *Verulamium, a Belgic and two Roman Cities*[8] is a milestone in the history of Romano-British studies since it represented the first successful attempt to write the history of a Romano-British town using excavated data as the primary source. The results provided a model for the history of Roman Verulamium (and for Romano-British towns in general) that was to influence Romano-British archaeology for at least a generation. Briefly this model was as follows. At the end of the late pre-Roman Iron Age, a settlement was established in Prae Wood on the edge of the plateau overlooking the Ver valley, half a kilometre west of the site that was to become the Roman town. After the conquest in AD 43, this settlement, consisting of 'rude and humble' dwellings, shifted down to the lower slopes of the valley. When the Boudiccan revolt broke out in AD 61, Verulamium was still little more than a collection of huts along Watling Street. The Wheelers found little that could be definitely associated with the destruction and burning in 61, and were it not for Tacitus' account of the sack of the town, it is doubtful that any mid-first-century catastrophe would have been detected. After the revolt a moderately sized town, covering approximately 100 acres (40ha), was established in the north-west half of the area later enclosed by the town walls. This was delimited by an earthwork defence known as the Fosse (**8**). The Wheelers suggested that the Fosse turned north at a point 240m west of the Silchester gate and ran down Bluehouse hill, at the time a deeply sunken lane. This, the 'first Roman city' of their report, they dated to the Hadrianic period. The Hadrianic town was succeeded by the second Roman city which was centred on the Forum and was surrounded by the town walls. These the Wheelers dated to the second century, partly on the basis of pottery sealed in or beneath the bank behind the town wall, and partly on the plans of the London and Chester Gates which resembled mid-second-century gateways on the Continent. This later second-century town contained high status houses with flint and mortar foundations, plastered and painted walls, tessellated floors and hypocausts; it

7 *Excavations in insula IV in 1932.* Copyright St Albans Museum

represented the peak of the town's development, but suffered a severe decline in the third century. The early fourth century saw a brief revival, referred to by the Wheelers as the 'Constantinian Renaissance'. This revival proved to be short-lived and by the middle of the fourth century the town was in rapid and terminal decline; the end of the century saw the inhabitants sinking to a condition of 'virtual barbarism'.

Today most elements in this 'Wheeler model' have been discarded, but at the time it marked a tremendous advance in the understanding, not only of the history of Verulamium, but of the development of Romano-British towns in general. The Wheelers' achievement can hardly be over emphasised. At a time when Roman pottery studies were still in their infancy, when aerial photography was only just beginning to be used, when many of the earthworks surrounding Verulamium had hardly been noticed, let alone surveyed, relying largely on untrained labour force, and without the aid of mechanical excavators or geophysics, they produced their classic report of the town. All this within six years of starting work.

The model suggested by the Wheelers was taken up by R.G. Collingwood, and subsequently by Ian Richmond, both of whom wrote classic syntheses of Roman Britain;[9] for more than 30 years after the Wheelers stopped excavating at Verulamium, the history of Roman Verulamium was seen as reflecting that of many of the towns, at least in the southern part of the province. This is hardly surprising. *Verulamium, a Belgic and Two Roman Cities* was the only published account of a Romano-British town that was based on the results of controlled excavation.

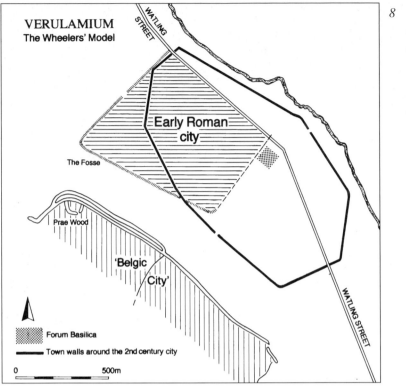

8　*The development of Verulamium as proposed by the Wheelers in 1936.* Drawn by David Williams

Although 1933 was the last year that the Wheelers themselves excavated in Verulamium, the following years saw further excavations by several of their colleagues and students. In 1934-5 Kathleen Kenyon and A.W.G. Lowther excavated the theatre and temple in insulae XV and XVI respectively (**9**), and in 1938 Miss K.M. Richardson excavated the *macellum* in insula XVII. Meanwhile, Norman Davey was excavating in the late first and early second-century cemetery half a kilometre south of the town on the brow of St Stephens Hill. In 1939 war once again brought archaeological excavation in the town to a close, and for the next ten years new finds were limited to chance discoveries made while digging gas pipe trenches or air raid shelters. Luckily the Verulamium Museum had been opened in 1939, and its first director was Philip Corder whose careful records ensured a steady trickle of new information throughout the war years.

In 1949 Mortimer Wheeler returned to Verulamium, this time assisted by Mrs Cotton and a team of students from the newly established Institute of Archaeology in London. Excavations were planned in the west corner of the Forum, but after excavating the temple near the west corner of the Forum court, the great depth of topsoil forced the team to turn their attention instead to a small building in the west corner of insula XIII.

1949 was to be Wheeler's final excavation at Verulamium and six years later the next chapter in the history of archaeology at Verulamium opened. Plans to construct a major road through the southern part of the Roman town had been mooted for many years, and were the subject of fierce debate as early as the 1930s. It was finally decided to build a

9 Kathleen Kenyon's excavations in the theatre in 1934. Copyright St Albans Museum

trunk road along the line of the existing Bluehouse Hill, at the time a narrow lane running along the north-west side of the Forum (**10** & **11**). The new road would cut a broad swathe through the Roman town, and would extend the line of the former lane across the previously undisturbed field in insula XVII. In 1955, in the face of this development, Sheppard Frere commenced a campaign of excavation that was to continue over seven summer seasons, and which would radically change the model of Verulamium's history proposed by the Wheelers.

In the 1930s the Wheelers had quickly realised that their excavations within the Roman town could only be properly interpreted in relation to the wider hinterland. They therefore excavated extensively in Prae Wood, and further afield at Wheathampstead. In much the same way, Sheppard Frere demonstrated that the results of excavations on the line of the new road could only be fully understood and explained in relation to the wider history of the town, and that many questions raised by the new excavation could only be resolved by excavating elsewhere. Consequently, as well as excavating the strip of land under and alongside the proposed road, a number of carefully targeted areas were examined at several other points in the town. These were primarily aimed at resolving the phases of the town defences, which themselves signalled the steady expansion of the town from the first to late third centuries. A summary account of the history of the Roman town, based on Frere's findings, was published in 1964 and the full results of the excavations were published between 1972 and 1984 in three monumental research reports.[10] The introduction to the second volume of the report outlined a new model for

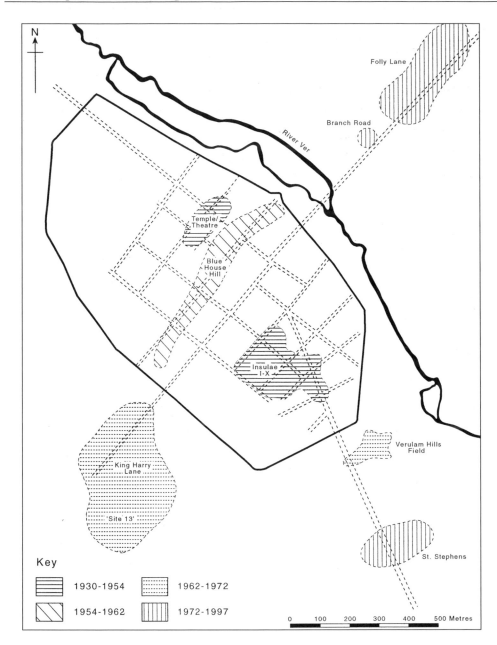

10 *Major excavations in Verulamium, 1930s-90s. The small excavations in the Forum/Basilica area are not included, but the almost total lack of excavation in the north and west parts of the Roman town is clear.* Drawn by Philip Dean

the history of the town. It differed radically from the Wheeler model, but like it, it had, and continues to have, a profound influence on a whole generation of Romano-British archaeologists. The radical differences between the Wheeler and Frere models were not entirely due to excavation; a chance discovery also played its part. In 1955, during building work in the playground of St Michael's school, a few metres north of the Roman Basilica, fragments of a monumental inscription were uncovered, and fortunately retrieved by the staff of the Verulamium Museum. These fragments almost certainly commemorated the completion of the Forum/Basilica complex, an event that the reconstructed text dated to AD 79.[11] A late first-century Basilica in this central position within the town clearly dealt a death blow to the Wheelers' suggestion that the post-Boudiccan town lay west of Bluehouse hill. The same year, 1955, also saw the discovery of a previously unsuspected defensive ditch. This ditch became known as the 1955 ditch, and was subsequently traced by geophysics and found to delimit an area of approximately 100 acres (40ha) around the Forum/Basilica. Excavation showed that the ditch was being gradually filled in during the first half of the second century, and it was concluded that the earthwork defence had originally been constructed in the mid-first century AD. All this placed the post-Boudiccan town firmly in the centre of the area later enclosed by the town walls, not to the west of Bluehouse Hill as had been suggested by the Wheelers. A final nail in the coffin of the Wheelers' model was the demonstration, after extensive excavation on the line of the new road, that the Fosse earthwork had never run north along the line of Bluehouse Hill. This made the whole idea of a Hadrianic town, enclosed by the Fosse and centred in the north-western part of the later town, completely untenable. The date of the town walls themselves was also revised. In the course of Frere's excavations four further trenches were cut through the bank behind the wall which showed that the wall could not be earlier than the late second century. The stratigraphical position of a coin hoard found on the site of the south-east tower was also reassessed and as a result the Wheelers' mid-second-century date for the walls was rejected in favour of one shortly before 375 (see p123 for a further discussion of the town walls). Inside the defences views about the development of the town itself changed just as radically. In the early 1960s many Romano-British towns were perceived as having developed around, or on the site of, conquest period forts. Verulamium was no exception. Frere explained the course of Watling Street in the southern part of Verulamium, where it cuts diagonally across the regular street grid, as being due to the fact that when originally laid out it was aiming at a Claudian fort somewhere between the site of the Forum and the river (**12**). The discovery on the north-east side of the town of a length of a rampart, revetted with turf and timber and dating to the Claudian period, provided powerful support to this theory, although the scarcity of Claudian coins from Verulamium generally suggested that any fort here had been short-lived. Frere suggested the core of the town, including the street grid, was established in the area around what was to become the Forum/Basilica, shortly after the abandonment of the fort in about 49. The initial date of the 1955 ditch was uncertain, but it was reasonable to suppose that it formed the boundary of this pre-Boudiccan town, although there was a possibility that it was not cut until shortly after 61. Within this town a row of workshops was built shortly after 50; Sheppard Frere suggested these had all been owned by a single landowner or entrepreneur, and worked by tenants or slaves. The workshops

11 *An aerial view of Sheppard Frere's excavations in 1955 prior to the widening of Bluehouse Hill in insulae XXI and XXII. Grids of excavation trenches are visible close to the hedge alongside the lane that preceded the modern road. The area of rough grass in the foreground overlies the south-west side of the Forum.* Reproduced courtesy of the St Albans Museum, copyright reserved

had all been destroyed in an intense fire which can be taken as evidence for the destruction of the town in 61.

In the course of the 1955-61 excavations it became clear that large tracts of Verulamium had been destroyed in another and previously quite unsuspected fire. This fire was initially dated to *c*.150, a date that was subsequently adjusted to the slightly later one of 155-60. The fire had swept through an area of at least 8ha in the north-west part of Verulamium, and resulted in extensive rebuilding in the later second century. There was little evidence in the 1955-61 excavations however for the widespread decline in the third century suggested by the Wheelers; on the contrary, building or rebuilding in insulae XX, XXII and XXVIII continued in the early third century. Equally work in the later 1950s failed to confirm a picture of widespread decay and the 'reversion to barbarism' that the

12 *The development*
   of Verulamium as
   proposed by
   Sheppard Frere.
   Drawn by
   David Williams

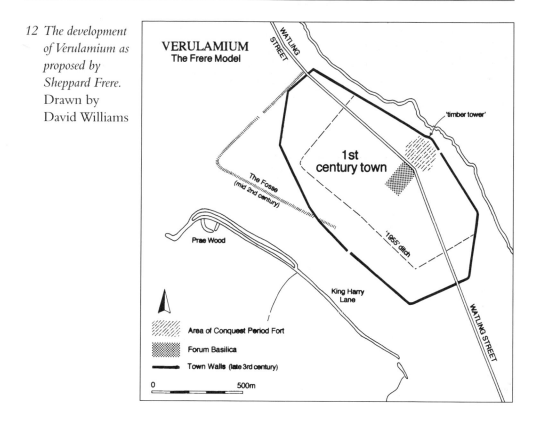

VERULAMIUM
The Frere Model

'timber tower'

1st
century town

The Fosse
(mid 2nd century)

'1955' ditch

Prae Wood

King Harry
Lane

▨ Area of Conquest Period Fort

▦ Forum Basilica

▬ Town Walls (late 3rd century)

0   500m

WATLING STREET

WATLING STREET

Wheelers had painted for the fourth-century town. Instead Sheppard Frere suggested that town life, including the provision of amenities such as a new water supply, continued in the centre of the town well into the fifth century.

The final season in the 'Frere campaign' of excavation was in 1961. Since then excavations within the town have tended to be restricted to smaller scale rescue work, usually in response to development in St Michael's village. These excavations were usually directed by staff from the Verulamium Museum, including Ilid Anthony, Chris Saunders, Adrian Havercroft, the author and Simon West. In all these excavations a significant part was also played by local volunteers, largely drawn from the 'Arch and Arch'. Much more extensive excavations took place in the suburbs and immediate hinterland of Verulamium. In the late '60s extensive rescue excavations under Ilid Anthony and Ian Stead took place on development sites immediately outside the town walls at Verulam Hills Field and King Harry Lane respectively. The most recent suburban excavation was directed by the author between 1991 and 1993 on the Folly Lane/Oysterfield site. Slightly further afield David Neal's excavations on villa sites to the south and west of Verulamium, and Jonathan Hunn's work on the development of historic landscapes in the area enabled the town to be viewed against its rural hinterland. Martin and Birthe Biddle have also conducted important excavations in the area around St Albans Abbey where they have revealed evidence for a late Roman cemetery, probably associated with an early Christian martyr's shrine. At the same time the development of geophysical methods (**13**), and the regular use of aerial surveys in the dry summers of the 1970s and early '80s added a new

13 An early geophysical survey tracing the course of the 1955 ditch in insulae V and VI in 1959.
Reproduced courtesy of the St Albans Museum, copyright reserved

dimension to the planning of the Roman town (**14**). In recent decades extensive excavation within the town walls has largely been replaced by area excavation on sites outside the walls. Today excavations within the town tend to be confined to very restricted and closely prescribed areas making it difficult to uncover meaningful plans, particularly of the late Roman deposits that are most at risk from disturbance. If carefully sited, a small trench may be able to resolve a specific question, although more often than not, even a small trench may raise more questions than it answers (**15**).

The large amount of rescue work that was undertaken both inside and outside the town walls in the 40 years since Sheppard Frere's excavations has not always been fully published. Although the amount of excavation has declined in recent years the need to analyse, sometimes reinterpret, and in many cases publish material preserved in the Verulamium Museum has seldom been greater. Some of this work has been done, but more of this, combined with geophysical surveys, would almost certainly throw as much new light on Verulamium's history as a further excavation.[12]

Before considering the evidence for the Roman town as it now appears, it is interesting to ask what progress has been made in our knowledge of Verulamium after a century of excavation, the majority of it carefully controlled and recorded. How have perceptions changed since Charles Bicknell and William Page started digging in the Vicarage grounds at the end of the nineteenth century? What are the questions that scholars ask today about the history and importance of Roman Verulamium? In this chapter the past models of the town's development have been reviewed — the late Victorian model, so deeply tinged by the imperialist attitudes of the time; the Wheeler concept, which still preserved a colonial flavour, one of barely civilised natives in contact with a superior, colonising power; and the more detailed Frere model, which saw a progressive development, during which the

14 Air photograph taken over Verulamium Park in the dry summer of 1976. The streets separating insulae III, IV, XI and XXIV on the east side of the Forum, are clearly marked by bands of parched grass.
Copyright St Albans Museum

town gradually changed over four centuries from a extramural settlement outside a conquest period fort to a 'residential, slightly sleepy, country town'.[13] The current model, which may or may not last as well, is set out in the following chapters.

What however are the differences in the questions that today's excavators hope to answer, compared to those of previous archaeologists? The late Victorians seem to have been concerned with the extent to which Verulamium corresponded to a Classical city; questions of the local economy, the surrounding countryside or the contribution of the local, native culture were not considered. The Wheelers sought to place Verulamium in the context of the surrounding landscape, and to relate it to the pre-existing population; hence their excavations in Prae Wood and at Beech Bottom Dyke and Wheathampstead in addition to those within the town. By the late 1950s and 1960s questions pre-occupying students of Roman Britain were more to do with elucidating the history of the province as a whole, setting it in the context of the wider Roman Empire, and understanding the whole process of 'Romanisation' of Britain. Specific aspects relating to the natural environment, the local economy and the activities of people within particular buildings, as opposed to the lives of the buildings themselves, were not questions that were considered in any detail in the reports on the Verulamium excavations, or indeed on most other Romano-British town excavations at the time. In the following chapters numerous questions will arise. Some will be those that previous excavators have grappled with, some will be new ones. In a few cases it is now necessary to modify interpretations based on

15 *A trench cut in 1986 to establish the line of Watling Street in insula XIII.* Copyright St Albans Museum

earlier work. In other areas new questions are being asked. For instance, almost nothing is known of the uses to which different rooms in domestic houses were put. The kind of families that lived in different houses remains a mystery; were houses occupied by small 'nuclear' families or by several related families? Were these tenants or 'owner occupiers'? In the past the paddocks, gardens, outbuildings and working areas with which most if not all the houses in the town must have been associated, have at best only received passing mention in excavation reports, and usually have been ignored by excavators altogether. There are frequent, passing references in past reports to property or plot boundaries usually in the form of small ditches or gullies, but occasionally described as 'garden walls'. Yet nothing is known about these plots themselves. Did they change over time, and how and when were buildings within them demolished and rebuilt? Increasingly this sort of question is being asked, alongside the 'old chestnuts' relating to the late Iron Age, the establishment of the 'Roman' town of Verulamium, its growth and decline during the centuries when it was a part of the Roman Empire, and the possible survival of a community here in the period after the collapse of Roman rule in Britain. In many cases however, it has to be admitted that answers to these questions, both old and new, seem as far away as ever.

2 The Catuvellauni at Verlamion

Verulamium lies on the south-eastern fringe of the Chiltern dip slope which in this area forms a chalk plateau, sloping gently down towards the east. The town grew up at the point at which the deposits of Clay with Flints and Plateau Drift which overlie the chalk plateau give way to the Boulder Clay in the Vale of St Albans. Although there is considerable local variation, broadly speaking the soils west of the town, derived from Clay with Flints, are heavy and acidic, while those over the Boulder Clay on the east are deeper, loamy and though rather more fertile are also heavy and badly drained. The plateau is cut by a number of small river valleys, flowing from the north-west to south-east. One of these is the Ver. Today this is a slow-moving, and very much shrunken stream, winding along a well-defined valley running from the source of the river 8km to the north, to its confluence with the river Colne, to the south of Colney Street, 8km to the south-east (**16**). The present-day river is often scarcely more than a trickle; this however is due to extraction of water in very recent times; in the medieval period it powered numerous mills, and in Roman and prehistoric times it was quite possibly navigable for flat-bottomed vessels. Numerous dry valleys lead into the Ver valley and on the valley slopes the underlying chalk is nearer the surface. This has resulted in lighter, better drained soils while those in the valley floors are different yet again, being derived from gravels laid down by melt water from glaciers at the end of the final ice age.

Until comparatively recently it was thought that at the time of the Roman conquest of southern England in AD 43, the area around Verulamium was still densely wooded. In the 1930s the Wheelers described the pre-Roman site in Prae Wood as being more or less in a clearing in woodland, the implication being that prior to *c.*10 BC settlement in the area was minimal. Today over 20 sites dating to the early first century AD are known within 10km of Verulamium, but as figure **17** demonstrates these are concentrated on the edge of the plateau and on the upper slopes of the river valleys, with large, apparently unoccupied areas between. While these intervening areas may have contained areas of woodland, environmental evidence suggests that at the time of the Roman conquest the landscape was dominated by pasture and arable land. The apparent absence of late Iron Age occupation on the plateau top may be due as much to the character of the local drift geology and lack of fieldwork as to anything else. The heavy, acid soils here are not particularly favourable to the preservation or detection of prehistoric pottery, nor are they conducive to the formation of crop marks enabling sites to be recognised from the air. Particularly illuminating in this respect is the recent discovery of an extensive late Iron Age site on a Clay with Flints area on the north slope of the Lea valley at Mackerye End. Here aerial photography and a fieldwalking survey in advance of a pipe-laying project in 1996 produced nothing apart from a single fragment of Romano-British tile. Nevertheless, geophysical survey and

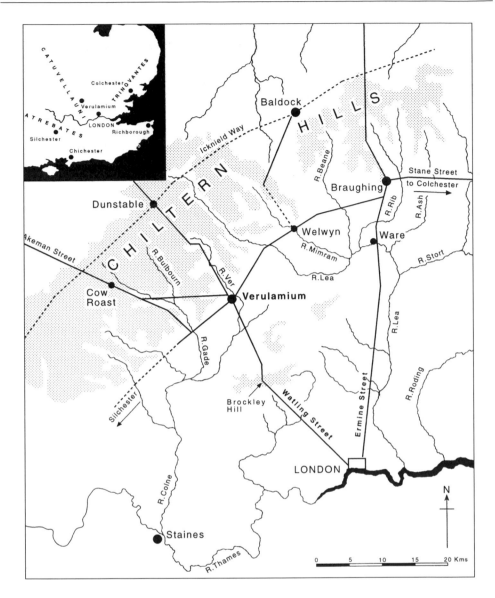

16 Verulamium in relation to major Roman roads and settlements in the area. Drawn by Philip Dean

subsequent excavation uncovered an extensive site, including substantial late Iron Age pits and ditches and remains of Romano-British masonry structures, all only a few centimetres beneath the modern ploughsoil. Also relevant in this context is recent work carried out on Berkhamsted Common, 15km west of Verulamium. This was common land in the medieval period, and has never been subjected to enclosure and ploughing to the extent usual elsewhere. As a result extensive remains of field systems, trackways, dykes and enclosures have survived to the present day. They were mapped in the 1980s.[1] Although no substantial excavation has been undertaken, significant quantities of late Iron Age and early Roman pottery have been collected and the amount of late Iron Age material in particular suggests that this part of the Chiltern plateau was already being settled in the immediately pre-Roman period. All this serves as a reminder that the widespread 'empty' areas around Verulamium may be more apparent than real.

The admittedly small quantity of environmental evidence that has been collected so far implies that by the middle of the first century AD only small areas of woodland survived. Pollen from waterlogged, peaty deposits in the flood plain of the river Ver, immediately north of the Roman town, suggested that by *c.*AD 50 the landscape upstream from the town was dominated, not by woodland species, but by those characteristic of grassland and arable fields.[2] This picture was confirmed in 1992 by studies of the pollen and the soil structure in the filling of a large, funerary shaft at Folly Lane, half a kilometre to the north-east of the town. This demonstrated that the shaft had been filled with soil brought from a wide variety of different locations, including heathland, marshy areas, and stockyards.[3] A similar picture was provided by the snail shells recovered during the excavation of the villa at Gorhambury, 2.5km west of Verulamium. Here mollusc shells sealed beneath earthworks dated to the final decades of the pre-Roman Iron Age were dominated by those of *Vallonia excentrica,* a species that prefers the open countryside and a relatively dry environment to a wooded, moist one.[4] Exactly when the forest cover was cleared is not so clear, but it is possible that some areas at least may already have been deforested for several centuries before the mid-first century AD. The question is an important one because the absence of all but residual woodland implies a substantial and well-established local population here at the end of the pre-Roman Iron Age in the first half of the first century AD. The immediate descendants of this population were (presumably) the people who built and occupied the earliest Roman town at Verulamium.

The end of the pre-Roman Iron Age

The first century BC had seen several innovations in south-east England. One of these was the introduction into the area of a new and easily recognised style of pottery, pottery that was increasingly produced using the potters' wheel. Vessels were made in a distinctive 'grog-tempered' fabric — that is using clay tempered with ground up fragments of other pots. A range of forms was produced, including pedestal jars, cordoned bowls and tazzas (cups) modelled on wooden prototypes. Another, slightly later change was indicated by the gradual spread of a new burial rite. Prior to the first century BC the rites for the disposal of the dead did not usually leave any trace detectable by archaeologists; bodies may have been exposed, or buried in rivers or marshes, or alternatively they have been cremated and the ashes simply scattered. From *c.*50 BC onwards however, it became increasingly common to cremate the dead and bury the ashes carefully, often contained in a pottery jar. These cremation burials were frequently accompanied by other 'offerings', usually pottery vessels (no doubt once containing food and drink), brooches, toilet articles such as mirrors, razors or nail cleaners, and animal remains. A few contained exceptionally rich offerings of pottery and metalwork, some of it imported from Italy and Gaul. These are the so-called princely or chieftain burials. North of the Thames they are concentrated in a band from north Essex and south Suffolk, across north Hertfordshire and south Cambridgeshire, and into Bedfordshire.

The 'ordinary' burials were frequently grouped in cemeteries. These were generally relatively small with only twenty or thirty cremation burials, suggesting that only a section of the population was buried in this way. There are also a few much larger cemeteries, notably one excavated in the 1960s immediately south of Verulamium at King Harry Lane. Here a total of 455 burials have been excavated, and dated to the period between the late first century BC and about AD 70. The overall number of late Iron Age cremation burials has enabled Ian Stead to divide them into two broad chronological divisions. His 'early', or Welwyn, group dates from *c.*50 BC-15 BC and is characterised by the appearance in the richer graves of pottery from central Gaul, Dressel Ib wine amphorae from Italy (and possibly Spain) and bronze and silver metalwork from Gaul and Italy. This is succeeded by the Lexden, or late phase, lasting from *c.*15 BC-AD 40. In this phase locally made pottery occurs alongside Arretine samian from north Italy, Dressel 20 amphorae from Spain, and fine, Gallo-Belgic tableware from northern and central Gaul.[5]

In the Verulamium area there is very little that can be confidently dated to the early, or Welwyn, phase. Indeed, over an area roughly covering the dip slope of the Chilterns south of the upper Lea valley, the introduction of grog-tempered wheel-turned pottery and cremation burials seems to have been delayed until the last decade of the first century BC. This is in marked contrast to the situation north of the upper Lea, in what today is north-east Hertfordshire and north-west Essex. Here imported pottery, locally made wheel-turned pottery in grog-tempered fabric, cremation burial and occasional chieftains' burials, all began to appear in the early first century BC.

A number of contemporary settlement sites are also known in this northern area. Baldock, 5km north of Hitchin, was a flourishing centre by the middle of the first century BC. Numerous dykes, sometimes making up multiple lines of banks and ditches were constructed, many of them running parallel to the trackway along the Chiltern scarp known as the Icknield Way. In the Iron Age the Icknield Way was an important trade route linking the middle Thames valley with the Wash. Other early trade routes also converged at Baldock. The most important of these was the route running through the Hitchin Gap to the Lea valley and thence to north Essex and ultimately the coast; after intersecting the Icknield Way this same route continued north-west to the Ouse valley and the Midlands. In the course of the first century BC an extensive network of ditched farmsteads separated by enclosures, paddocks and trackways grew up around this intersection. Dykes were constructed, probably with a view to channelling movement into the centre of the settlement area, which today lies beneath the centre of modern Baldock.[6] Away from this central area, traces of occupation and lengths of linear ditches extend across approximately 12km². Cemeteries were strung out along the crest of the Chiltern escarpment on the northern edge of the main settlement area. These contained both inhumation and cremation burials, some of them within ditched and banked enclosures. A few burials were exceptionally wealthy, and two can be classed as chieftains' burials. Both date to the first half of the first century BC, and are among the earliest late Iron Age remains from Baldock. Overall, material from the burials and from areas of settlement suggest that the local community here was a prosperous one, steadily increasing in size from the last quarter of the first century BC until the time of the Roman conquest.

The pre-eminent centre in the area, however, lay 16km south-east of Baldock at Braughing. Here occupation grew up on either side of the river Rib, a tributary of the Lea. With easy communications with the Thames valley (via the Rib and Lea), the chalk uplands of north Hertfordshire and Cambridgeshire, and the rich farmland of north-west Essex there can be little doubt that Braughing was another settlement that owed its importance in the late Iron Age to its role as a route centre. Earthwork defences on rising ground at Gatesbury, overlooking the valley of the Rib 0.5km south-east of the modern village of Braughing, have not been satisfactorily dated, although finds from the site suggest occupation here in the second half of the first century BC. Pre-Roman settlement has also been recorded on Wicham Hill and on low-lying ground both to the north-west and south of Gatesbury. In all, traces of occupation have been found over at least 100ha, although not all of this enormous area was occupied simultaneously. Excavations in the 1970s and early 1980s found evidence of a dramatic surge in the population in about 20-15 BC and the focus of the settlement generally seems to have shifted in the course of the half century leading up to the Roman conquest. One such focus lay at Skeleton Green, on the east bank of the river, where remains of nine rectangular timber buildings were excavated in 1971. These were occupied from *c*.15 BC to AD 45 although there was apparently a hiatus in occupation between about AD 20-35. So far these late Iron Age buildings are without parallel in the area and it has been suggested that they represent a trading community, perhaps of Gallic merchants. There is certainly a remarkably high concentration of imported pottery from Braughing, greater quantities of Gallic and Italian imports have been recorded here than from any other site in either Hertfordshire or Essex.[7]

Baldock and Braughing were by no means the only late Iron Age settlements in the area however. Occupation sites dating back to the same period have been found all across the area drained by the small rivers feeding into the upper Lea from the north. There appears to have been a particular concentration around Welwyn where fieldwork has revealed extensive occupation from the mid-first century BC onwards.

Verlamion at the end of the pre-Roman Iron Age

Before embarking on a discussion of the late Iron Age predecessor of Roman Verulamium, it is important to explain variations in the town's name. A mint mark on late pre-Roman Iron Age coins refers to the place as Verlamio, which is presumed to be from the Greek Verlamion. On the other hand Tacitus refers to the Roman town as Verulamio (the Latin locative). Later Roman sources refer to it as Verolamion or Virolamium. This has led to the development of a convention in recent academic literature to refer to the pre-conquest settlement as Verlamion, and the post-conquest town as Verulamium. Although there is in reality considerable doubt about the actual spelling of the name in the Roman period, let alone before the conquest, this convention is a convenient way of referring to the rather different types of settlement that existed here before and after the conquest. It is consequently the convention that has been adopted in this book.

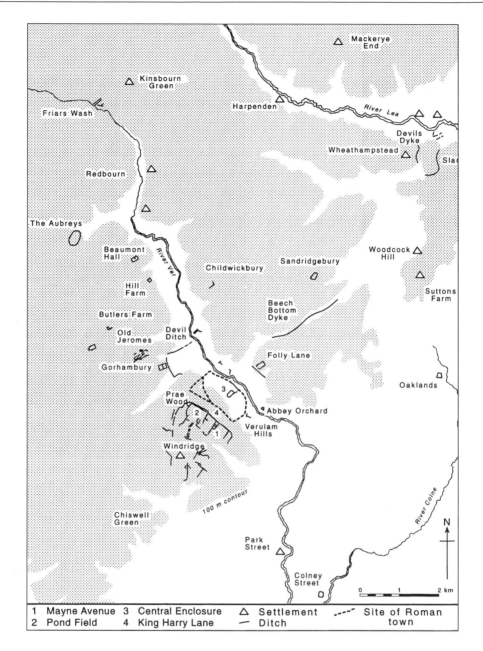

17 The Verulamium area in the late pre-Roman Iron Age. Drawn by Philip Dean

So far no rich burials or extensive settlements dating from the first century BC have been found in the Verlamion area, and knowledge of precisely what if anything was going on here is still very much a matter for speculation. Even the dates at which grog-tempered and wheel-turned pottery were introduced into the area are unclear, although dates in the first half of the first century BC have been suggested for wheel-turned pottery at

Wheathampstead, on the south side of the Lea, 7.5km north of Verlamion. An early (Neuheim) type of brooch from silt that collected in the base of the massive Devils Dyke that formed the western boundary of the site, supports the suggestion of an early start to occupation here (**colour plate 3**). Pottery from an occupation site at Sutton's Farm, 4km north of Verlamion may also date from a similar period, as it did not contain any vessels influenced by Continental styles characteristic of the Lexden phase. The total quantity of pottery from this site however was small, and this point cannot be taken as conclusive evidence for settlement here in the mid-first century BC. It is also worth noting that once imported into north Hertfordshire and north-west Essex the luxury tableware and amphorae appear to have been monopolised by only a small section of contemporary society — presumably some sort of social elite. Much of the imported material is connected with the ostentatious consumption of food and drink and is found in princely burials and at Braughing. It does not seem to have been distributed through the population at large. It may be simply the result of chance that elite settlement sites or burials dating from the Welwyn phase have not yet been found in the Verulamium area. It would only take a few such sites to radically alter these apparent differences between the areas north and south of the upper Lea.

Another unknown factor is exactly what sort of social changes lie behind the appearance of these new types of pottery and burial rites. The gradual spread of new burial practices implies a fairly radical change in what in all societies is an important 'rite of passage'. On the other hand, the adoption of novel pottery styles may not reflect much more than a change of fashion, a fashion moreover that was taken up more readily by some families and groups than by others. The picture suggested by pollen evidence of a contemporary landscape dominated by pasture or cereal crops, implies a numerous and well-established population. Sadly these people have left little trace in the archaeological record. The pottery they produced here in the early Iron Age was made in a fabric tempered with flint grits. Small fragments of it are frequently found on late Iron Age and early Roman sites in the St Albans area, often scattered in the topsoil or surviving as rubbish in later deposits. Conventionally this pottery is dated to between the eighth and sixth centuries BC. In addition to flint-gritted pottery a very few sites have produced rather finer sherds in 'Middle Iron Age sandy ware'. In 1970 fragments from several such vessels were recovered from widespread contexts in the course of building operations on a site immediately adjacent to the King Harry Lane cemetery. These vessels survived in large, and obviously unweathered fragments and clearly indicate a nearby settlement in the early first century BC if not earlier.[8] More recently pottery described as 'middle Iron Age' has been recorded in evaluation excavations at Oaklands College and Leavesden airfield, both within 15km of Verulamium. The tiny and beautifully decorated bronze knife, found by chance about a kilometre south of Verulamium and dating on stylistic grounds to the second or third century BC, provides a vivid illustration of the quality of metalwork produced in the area (**colour plate 4**).

A common feature in the pre-Roman, Iron Age landscape around St Albans are enclosures surrounded by ditches and banks. On the whole the banks have weathered, or been ploughed away and the ditches (generally less than 2m deep) have long since become completely silted up and are only visible in dry summers as crop marks. The enclosures vary between 0.6-2ha and are normally sited on the upper slope of valleys, near the edge of the Clay with Flints plateau. Although they occur north of the upper Lea, and indeed are known from right across the Chiltern dip slope, they seem to occur with particular frequency along the valley of the Ver. Including two rather doubtful examples north-west of Redbourn, 17 have been recorded in the Ver valley between its source near Flamstead and its confluence with the Colne at Colney Street. Most are rectilinear in plan, but four are curvilinear, and two more have substantial curvilinear elements as part of a complex system of ditches, probably of differing dates.

Only on five sites in the Ver valley (Parkbury, Oaklands, Gorhambury, Mayne Avenue and Redbourn by-pass) and on two probable examples in the Lea valley (Mackerye End and Wick Avenue, Wheathampstead) has any excavation been carried out. On all these sites evidence was found for rectilinear or sub-rectangular enclosures with late Iron Age, wheel-made and grog-tempered pottery in the primary fills of the ditches. So far no controlled excavation has been undertaken on the less regular, curvilinear enclosures. These are less numerous than the rectilinear examples and may be rather earlier in date. Thus while it may be that the rectilinear enclosures are typical of the century before the Roman conquest, the more irregular and curvilinear earthworks may prove to belong to a slightly earlier period. It is worth noting in this connection the remains of a curvilinear enclosure to the south of the King Harry Lane cemetery, which appears to have been associated with the middle Iron Age sherds mentioned above.

A notable and obvious exception to the normal pattern of earthwork enclosures is the Aubreys earthwork, 6.5km north-west of Verulamium. Here substantial earthworks enclose a roughly oval area covering 9ha with one entrance on the west and another smaller one on the north-west. The Aubreys lies on the edge of the plateau at the head of a small dry valley running into the Ver valley. In spite of several small-scale excavations both inside the earthwork and on the defences, no firm dating evidence has been recovered so the date and purpose of the earthwork remain unclear.

Compared to the occupation in the valleys, settlement on the top of the Clay with Flints plateau appears to have been sparse (**17**). This may simply be the result of differential fieldwork, or the difficulty of recognising sites in the heavier clay soils that predominate here. On the other hand, intensive surveys elsewhere in Hertfordshire have indicated a preference for the upper slopes around the edge of the clay plateau as sites for settlement both in the late Iron Age and in the Roman period. A likely explanation for this is that the slopes of the valley were used for arable farming, while the heavier, less fertile soils on the plateau top provided pasture for cattle and horses. Farmers established on the upper slopes were consequently best placed for exploiting both types of soil.

So far little mention has been made of another major element in the late pre-Roman Iron Age scene — coinage. Coinage was first introduced into southern England in the second century BC, when gold coins were imported from Gaul. Between about 80 and 10 BC the quantity of coins imported from Gaul increased substantially, and increasingly included silver as well as gold; by the end of the first century BC bronze coins were also being brought into the area. Not only were these coins coming into the country but they were extensively copied here, giving rise to a variety of local, British types. By the end of the first century BC these British coins were increasingly influenced by Roman prototypes, and for the first time inscribed British coins appeared.

Locally the distribution of coins in the first century BC confirms the impression of differences between the Verlamion area and that further north.[9] In his definitive study of late Iron Age coinage, Colin Haselgrove pointed out that while in the north-east Chilterns and east Hertfordshire there were significantly more coins dating from the first century BC than from the early first century AD, in the south-west Chilterns the ratios were exactly the opposite. In the southern Chilterns gold coins continued as the principal coinage in use at a time when further north, British bronze coins were being produced and lost in substantial quantities, particularly at sites like Braughing. This led Haselgrove to suggest that in the later first century BC there were two distinct areas, one in the north Chilterns and East Hertfordshire, an area including the Baldock, Braughing and Welwyn sites, and the other in the south-west Chilterns. Verlamion, while within this latter area, was close to the boundary between the two; it is not difficult to see the upper Lea valley as defining the frontier between the two territories.

Although the absence of imported goods does not necessarily mean that the population in the Verlamion area was sparse or impoverished, it does appear that for much of the first century BC the people here did not readily adopt the innovations in coinage, pottery styles and burial rites that were so marked a feature on contemporary sites further north. Even in the northern Chilterns however, these innovatory traits may well have been confined to a small, and presumably elite, section of society. On the other hand it suggests that the area that in the Roman period was to form the Catuvellaunian *civitas* was originally occupied by at least two rather different groups. North of the Lea an elite social group obtained and monopolised exotic goods from the Continent. South of the Lea elite groups (if they existed) were more conservative in their tastes. Whether this was from choice or necessity we cannot tell.

Verlamion in the early first century AD

The difference between the two areas disappeared in the early first century AD. Starting in about 20-15 BC, grog-tempered and wheel-turned pottery made its appearance at Verlamion, along with cremation burial in flat cemeteries and material characteristic of Stead's 'Lexden' phase. This was accompanied by the use in the south-west Chilterns of locally made, inscribed gold, silver and bronze coins.

The appearance of well fired, grog-tempered pottery makes it much easier to recognise archaeological sites. This in turn has allowed a substantial number of settlement sites in the Verlamion area to be dated with a fair degree of confidence, to the 50 or 60 years before the Roman conquest. Currently about 25 of these sites are known in the Ver, Colne and upper Lea valley, while at the same time in the upper Bulbourne valley, near Berkhamsted Common and Cow Roast, 15km west of Verlamion, iron working commenced on a massive scale. Verlamion itself now appears as the focus of a concentration of sites although it is important to bear in mind the disproportionate amount of fieldwork that has taken place here which may have distorted the true picture.

The Wheelers in their pioneering excavations in the early 1930s were the first to demonstrate the presence of a pre-conquest occupation site at Prae Wood, on the edge of

18 Prae Wood during excavations in 1931. Copyright St Albans Museum

the Clay with Flints plateau, now in private land half a kilometre south-west of the Roman town (**18**). This they identified as the site of pre-conquest Verlamion, and interpreted the small, sub-rectangular ditched enclosure at the west end of a linear dyke along the plateau edge as a royal residence (**19**). In the 1970s and 1980s however, air photography by the Verulamium Museum staff, and field surveys by Jonathan Hunn, showed conclusively that pre-Roman occupation had spread across extensive areas of the plateau south of the Roman town; by the early 1990s it had become clear that similar occupation existed on the north side of the valley as well.[10]

It now appears that Prae Wood, far from being the centre of the pre-Roman occupation, was only a small element in a much wider pattern of settlement (**19**). It is even possible to detect a pattern emerging. At the edge of the plateau were linear dykes represented by the Wheeler Ditch, New Dyke and the Folly Lane ditch. These were 1.5m or more deep, with the bank on the downhill side. Behind these were ditched enclosures, compounds and drove ways, all suggestive of occupation sites and farms. Unfortunately remains of structures within the enclosures are elusive. All these sites have been severely eroded, and this, combined with the acid soil conditions, has all too frequently destroyed all traces of timber structures and stratified deposits. Often all that remains are the truncated bases of ditches and pits, and it is difficult to do much more than recover the plans of the enclosures, and with luck estimate their date. Most enclosures were elongated rectangles and in a few instances they were subdivided between an inner and outer compound. In the few examples that have been excavated, traces of industrial activities have been recorded. Triangular clay loomweights have been recorded from Prae Wood and Folly Lane, and pottery kilns or ovens from Prae Wood and Pond Field.

Only at Gorhambury, 1.5km west of Prae Wood and excavated by David Neal in the 1980s, have traces of pre-Roman buildings been found within one of these enclosures.[11] The villa that had occupied the site during the Roman period had inevitably removed many traces of earlier occupation, but nevertheless it was possible to distinguish three phases of occupation between about 10 BC and AD 60. As on so many local sites, a scatter of flint-gritted pottery suggested a certain amount of earlier Iron Age occupation here but it was not until the very end of the first century BC that a rectangular ditched enclosure (enclosure A) was constructed (Gorhambury phase 3). A track or droveway defined by V-shaped ditches (the antennae ditches) led into the enclosure from the south-west. The primary silt in one of these contained a small collection of grog-tempered pottery and a coin of Cunobelin (see below p52) which allowed the excavators to date the enclosure to within the first half of the first century AD. Not long after its completion enclosure A was extended (phase 4) and an imposing timber gateway constructed at its western entrance, with a rather more modest one on the east. Phase 5 saw the conversion of the phase 4 extension into a south-western or inner enclosure, enclosure B.

Within these two enclosures traces of 12 buildings were identified. They were dated to the first half of the first century AD, although it was not possible to assign them to a particular phase within this general period with any degree of certainty. Both round and rectangular buildings were represented, constructed in a variety of ways. Altogether the buildings comprised two rectangular houses, one of them with at least two rooms (the so-called 'proto villa'), three rectangular huts, two round huts, a large rectangular barn, a flint-lined tank, one (possibly two) granaries and an 'unidentified structure'. Several of the buildings rested on timber cill beams, while others relied on earth-fast posts. Chalk and beaten earth floors were common as was cob walling. The 'proto villa' may have included a wing, forming an L-shaped house; its cob walls were unusual in being contained between wattles and are reminiscent of the 'double' walls that revetted the sides of the Folly Lane funerary shaft (see below p46). Most of the buildings at Gorhambury were found in enclosure B, which was the part of the site destined to become the site of the Roman villa at the end of the first century AD. As in the Roman period, enclosure A was less densely occupied and substantial parts of it were presumably reserved for livestock. The main building recognised in this enclosure was a large aisled building. This, the excavators considered, had probably been used to house estate workers and livestock, or as a store.

It is clear that even in the pre-Roman period Gorhambury was a high status site. Comparatively large numbers of pre-Roman coins and early brooches were found here and the 'proto villa' contained an early *mortarium* (a heavy ceramic bowl, gritted on the interior, and used for grinding ingredients), suggesting that Roman styles of food preparation were already being practised here in the pre-conquest period. A deposit in the same building produced seeds of coriander and fig as well as those of native fruits — blackberry and sloe. All this suggests wealthy occupants, capable of importing exotic goods and implying a higher status for the owner of Gorhambury than that enjoyed by the inhabitants of the Prae Wood settlement. Until more enclosures are excavated however, it is impossible to say whether Prae Wood or Gorhambury is more typical of the area.

The Dykes

Today the most striking remains of pre-Roman Verlamion are the massive earthworks that still survive on the west of modern St Albans. Undoubtedly the most impressive of these is the Beech Bottom Dyke (**colour plate 5**). The most dramatic stretch of this dyke lies on the east of the Harpenden road where there are still traces of low banks on either side of a 30m wide ditch. It has never been excavated, but its existing depth of nearly 10m suggests that originally it was something in the order of 12-13m deep. The course of this dyke, and indeed its purpose, is still not entirely clear. In spite of the tremendous effort that must have been required to construct it, it was clearly never intended as a defensive work. The existing length runs for 1.5km along the floor of a dry valley, overlooked by higher ground on both sides, and this, together with its very length, means that it could never have been effectively defended. It is possible that it was designed to define the route between Verulamium and Wheathampstead, in much the same way as the Baldock dykes probably channelled movement along the Chiltern scarp and into the main settlement area. Fieldwork has failed to find anything to suggest that the Beech Bottom Dyke ever formed a continuous earthwork linking the Ver valley with the Devils Dyke and the Lea valley, and it is clear that neither dyke ever extended beyond the head of their respective dry valleys (**17**). Any boundary defining a route across the intervening area must have been marked by less permanent means such as hedges or palisades.

The date of the Beech Bottom Dyke is also uncertain. While the Devils Dyke may well have been cut in the mid-first century BC, the only dating evidence for the Beech Bottom earthwork is that provided by a coin hoard, found during road works in the Harpenden road in 1932. A hoard of 41 Roman *denarii* had been buried in the ditch at a time when at least 3m of silt had already accumulated in it. The latest coin in the hoard was one of Hadrian, minted in 118.

What may be a continuation of the Beech Bottom Dyke south of the Ver is represented by the Devils Ditch. Here again no complete section has ever been excavated across the earthwork. Nevertheless is it possible to date the Devils Ditch with rather more precision than is possible for the Beech Bottom dyke. The high status site at Gorhambury (described above) lay within a few metres of the south-eastern arm of the Devils Ditch, the so-called New Dyke. Throughout periods 3 and 4 of the site's history, spanning the early decades of the first century AD, the New Dyke did not exist; it was not until the conversion of the earlier farmstead into a double enclosure in period 5 that the earthwork was constructed to the north of it. Furthermore it is clear that the earthwork was carefully planned so as to incorporate Gorhambury into the overall scheme. An original causeway was left leading across the New

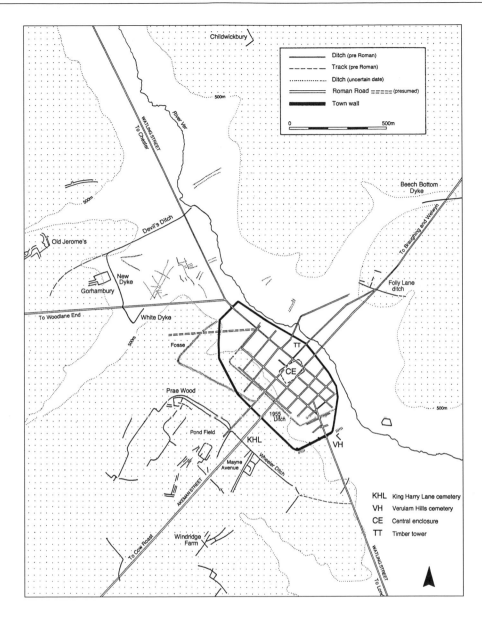

19 The Verlamion oppidum in the early first century AD also showing Roman town and roads.
  Drawn by David Williams

Dyke ditch giving direct access to the principal timber gateway into the farmstead which was now moved from the west side of the enclosure to the east. Unfortunately the initial date of Gorhambury period 5 is not absolutely certain. While it quite possibly dates from sometime at the end of the pre-Roman period, it may equally well have only commenced shortly after the conquest. This in turn could mean that the Beech Bottom Dyke and the Devils Ditch were also only completed in the middle years of the first century AD.

Although Beech Bottom Dyke and the Devils Ditch/New Dyke were the largest of the Verlamion earthworks, smaller ditches divided the area west and south of the Roman town into a number of different sized blocks. The largest of these ditches was the White Dyke, discovered during the Gorhambury excavations, with an overall width of 23m (including the ditch and the bank on its southern side). This earthwork ran for 250m roughly parallel to the Devils Ditch and nearly 400m south of it; the south-western ends of the two earthworks were linked by the New Dyke. Somewhat less substantial linear dykes defined the edge of the plateau; to the south of the river these are represented by the Prae Wood and Wheeler ditches, and on the north by the Folly Lane ditch. On the upper, plateau side of these plateau edge ditches, a series of cross-country ditches and palisades divided the area into roughly rectangular blocks. Today all these ditches are totally buried, but originally they were at least 1.5m deep. The accompanying banks were on their downhill sides, but together they would have formed a significant barrier, certainly sufficient to have confined livestock and define property boundaries. The linear, plateau edge ditches seem to have marked the boundary between the valley slopes and floor and the higher ground on top of the plateau. It is striking that with one exception the 'farmstead' enclosures were confined to the uphill side of the linear ditches, which cut them off from the valley. This is emphasised by the position of the entrances that were sited to allow access from the plateau, but not from the valley (**19**). Even at Gorhambury it was only in period 5 that the main access to the site was from the valley rather than from the plateau. Certainly the linear ditches on the plateau edge were dug rather earlier than the New Dyke, and possibly also than the Devils Ditch and Beech Bottom Dyke; excavations on the Prae Wood Ditch, Wheeler Ditch and Folly Lane Ditch all suggest that they were originally cut early in the first century AD if not before. On the other hand there is some evidence suggesting that both the New Dyke and the White Dyke overlie earlier boundary ditches, ditches which may be contemporary with those at Prae Wood and Folly Lane.[12]

In the area that was to become the centre of the Roman town, in the valley floor, the pre-Roman land-use was rather different. The Roman Forum/Basilica complex overlies a large enclosure, the Central Enclosure, about 2ha in extent, and surrounded by an unusually substantial ditch. The Central Enclosure was first recognised in 1955 in two places. Its north-eastern corner was located under the museum car park, and the south-western in insula XXVII, 15m west of the south end of the Forum. The line of the remainder of the Central Enclosure's ditch is largely conjectural, but the presence of deeply disturbed deposits under the north-east side of the Basilica and also under one of the temples in the south-west side of the Forum give a reasonable indication of its likely course (**19 & 31**). Several small excavations have suggested that another arm of the ditch ran north towards the river, and Simon West has recently confirmed this during excavations on the site of a proposed extension to the Museum.[13] None of the ditches in this area seem to have been filled in until at least 20 years after the Roman conquest, and though their initial date is not known, the ditch beneath the Forum at least appears to have already been silting up in the middle of the first century and so must have been dug sometime earlier.

The area immediately to the west and north of the Central Enclosure has produced substantial numbers of mould slabs. These slabs, often referred to in the past as coin moulds, consisted of rectangular slabs of fired clay with rows of similarly sized cylindrical impressions. The impressions sometimes contain traces of gold, silver or bronze, and occasionally isolated plugs of metal. While no longer thought to be moulds for coin blanks, they were probably used for producing metal lumps of standardised weights, such as could have been used, among other things for the production of coins. They occur on high-status sites, and Verulamium has produced particularly large concentrations of them, including the practically complete example illustrated in plate 20. Coins of both Tasciovanus and Cunobelin include the name or Vir or Verlamio implying that Verlamion was the site of a mint. The whole question of the coins and the 'dynasty' that produced them is discussed below, but it is important to note here the concentration of slab moulds around

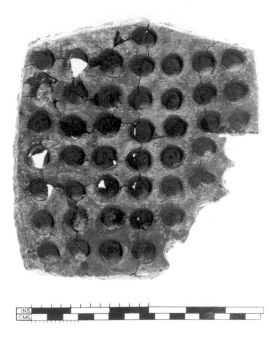

20 A nearly complete clay slab mould, with moulds from 50 pellets arranged in seven rows of seven, with an extra one at the top. Found in 1957 in Insula XXV. Copyright St Albans Museum

the area that was to become the site of the Forum/Basilica complex in Roman Verulamium, a concentration that suggests that this was already an important site in the early first century AD. As Sheppard Frere suggested many years ago, it may have been the site of the pre-Roman mint, perhaps associated with a 'royal' residence or 'kraal'.[14]

An alternative interpretation for the Central Enclosure is as a ceremonial or religious site. The early first century AD was a time when specifically ritual sites appear in the area. At Essenden, 14km north-east of Verlamion, an irregular ditched enclosure demarcated what was almost certainly a sacred area where spears, swords, coins, ingots and a fragment of at least one torc were deposited in the first centuries BC and AD.[15] Still closer to Verlamion near the source of the river Ver at Friars Wash a triple dyke, almost certainly dating to the late pre-Roman Iron Age, delimited an area that later became an important Romano-British cult site (*see* **56**).

With the exception of the site at Folly Lane, pre-Roman burials were confined either to the valley floor or to its slopes, on the downhill sides of the plateau edge ditches; as yet none has been recorded from the plateau top itself. Pre-Roman and conquest period cemeteries are known at King Harry Lane, St Stephens, Verulam Hills Field and beneath insula XXVIII of the Roman town. In 1968-70 Ian Stead excavated the large cemetery at King Harry Lane, just south of the Roman town. Here he recorded 455 cremations and 17 inhumations making the site the largest late Iron Age cemetery so far excavated in this

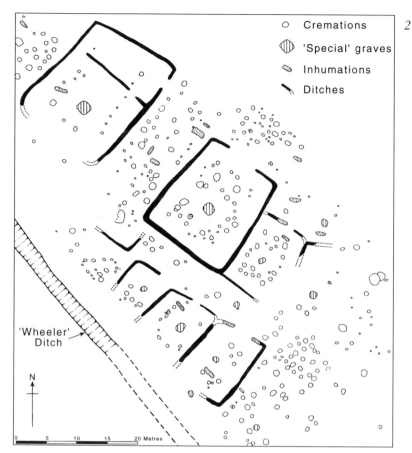

Cremations ○
'Special' graves ⦾
Inhumations ⬤
Ditches ⬚

'Wheeler' Ditch

N

0   5   10   15   20 Metres

21 Plan of part of the late Iron Age cemetery at King Harry Lane. After Stead and Rigby, drawn by Philip Dean

country. The cemetery included traces of 8 ditched burial enclosures, each covering between 120-300m², and three further 'clusters' of burials which may once have been enclosed by ditches which have since been weathered away (**21**). The cemetery was originally dated to between 10 BC and AD 60, but this dating has been questioned recently and some scholars now prefer a date of around 20 or even 25 BC for the earliest burials, and a correspondingly earlier 'end date' of *c*.AD 43 for the latest.[16] Stead suggested that the King Harry Lane cemetery represented the inhabitants of the Prae Wood settlement. In the 1960s however, permission to excavate was only given on half of the site. Subsequent building operations were watched by members of the local archaeological society who were able to demonstrate that not only did the King Harry Lane cemetery extend further to the east, where later first-century burials may have concentrated, but also that there were also extensive areas of occupation immediately adjacent to the cemetery, on the other side of the Wheeler ditch. The settlement or settlements that the cemetery served remains uncertain. In any case the recorded burials are unlikely to represent the entire local community, and may well be those of people drawn from a comparatively small, elite, social group.

Many of the central burials within the enclosures or burial groups were distinguished by the inclusion of more numerous or elaborate grave offerings. As well as these more or

22 *Mid-first-century inhumation burials in the cemetery enclosure ditch at Verulam Hills Field.* Copyright St Albans Museum

less intact grave offerings, however, the central burials all included varying proportions of burnt 'pyre offerings', that is the burnt remains of objects that had been burnt with the body on the funeral pyre. This suggests that a rather different funerary rite had been afforded to the individuals buried at the centres of enclosures. Since these central graves included at least one of an immature youth they cannot represent the founding members of families; nevertheless, they are presumed to be the graves of some sort of special group within the community.

Most of the excavated burials of this date were cremation burials, but there were in addition a significant number of inhumations. Unlike the cremation burials which were normally accompanied by pottery, brooches and food offerings, the inhumations were almost invariably unaccompanied by any grave goods. They were apparently simply laid in the bases of the ditches around the enclosures or in the banks next to them; there was a marked preference for these burials to be placed near the entrances into the burial enclosures (**21** & **22**).

Other burial enclosures have been recorded at Verulam Hills Field and St Stephens, although none has been completely excavated. By and large it appears that the larger the enclosure the fewer the numbers of burials within it. This is demonstrated *par excellence* by a burial on the north side of the river, at Folly Lane. Although dating from a few years after the Roman conquest it clearly belongs to the established, indigenous, pre-Roman funerary tradition. At Folly Lane the cremation burial, accompanied by the burnt remnants of an exceptionally rich collection of pyre goods, appears to have been the sole cremation burial within a rectangular burial enclosure covering nearly 2ha. There was also clear evidence that the burial of the cremated remains was simply the final act in a remarkably complex, and probably long drawn out, funerary ritual. This had involved the construction of a sunken funerary chamber on the floor of a large pit or shaft, approximately 3m deep and revetted with clay and gravel tamped down between a double timber wall. On the floor of the shaft were the scattered fragments of what had been a large collection of tableware, comprising at least 32 vessels (mainly cups and platters) and including a substantial number of vessels imported from Gaul. Sherds from Italian wine amphorae implied that a large quantity of wine had also been consumed and the overall impression was that a funeral feast or wake had been held, either in the funerary shaft itself, or close by. This impression was supported by fragments of furniture, including remains of a firedog, and a small silver handle, that were found mixed with the pottery. Perhaps the most plausible explanation of the shaft is as a place where the corpse was exposed, or 'lay in state' before finally being cremated. How long this period lasted is impossible to say, but it is reasonable to assume that it culminated in a funerary feast, after which the body was finally cremated in the centre of the enclosure, a few metres west of the funerary shaft. It had been accompanied on the pyre by a large collection of expensive and 'showy' objects, including at least 2.5kg of silver (which only survived as solidified lumps of molten metal), bronze and enamel horse gear (**colour plate 6**), remains of an ivory mounted couch or chair and a complete tunic of iron mail (**25**). A token quantity of the pyre debris and fire-damaged pyre goods was then buried in a shallow pit immediately north of the funerary shaft together with a small proportion of the cremated human remains. The funerary chamber was then deliberately demolished, and both the funerary shaft and the burial pit filled and covered by a turf stack. The site of the pyre itself was carefully marked by a standing post, and at the entrance to the enclosure three human inhumations were laid on the base of the butt end of the ditch. The Folly Lane burial is so far unique in its position on the uphill side of a plateau edge ditch, a position, which together with the size of the enclosure and wealth of the pyre goods, underlines the exceptional character of the burial, and, presumably, the outstanding importance of the man whose remains were buried here.[17]

The Verlamion *oppidum* at the time of the conquest

One characteristic of the late pre-Roman Iron Age in southern Britain was the appearance in the course of the first century BC of a new type of settlement, known as *oppida*. These settlements varied considerably but shared a number of common features. They formed extensive complexes extending over areas of up to 32km² (12.5 square miles). Within these areas different foci tended to develop with industrial and commercial areas separated from occupation, ceremonial and burial areas. *Oppida* generally included substantial dykes and frequently produce evidence for high status metalworking. There is considerable discussion as to the origin of *oppida*; some may have started life as meeting places for different tribal groups, they may have grown up around an aristocratic residence, or they may have been primarily ritual centres.

Verlamion has been recognised as an *oppidum* since the Wheelers' work here in the 1930s. By the time of the Roman conquest it was the focus of a well-populated area in which farmsteads and their associated compounds were strung out along the edge of the plateau along the whole length of the Ver valley (**17**). A similar pattern of occupation may well have operated in the valleys of the Lea and Gade to the north and south respectively, although much more fieldwork needs to be undertaken in these areas before the relative importance of occupation in the different valleys becomes clear. As mentioned above, the extent to which the intervening plateau areas were settled is also still unclear.

As in other *oppida* Verlamion shows clear evidence for careful zoning in the use of land. Not only were most farmsteads cut off from the cemeteries on the valley slopes, but different types of industrial activity were also separated. Weaving and pottery production took place in, or close to, occupation sites on the plateau edge while bronze, silver and gold working was carried out on the lower slopes or in the valley floor as it is here that most (although not quite all) slab moulds have been found.

As always the people themselves remain elusive. The acid soil, which all too often destroys bones, combined with the prevalence of cremation burial at the end of the Iron Age, means that there is little skeletal material to turn to. The inhumations in the ditches of funerary enclosures at Verulam Hills Field and Folly Lane give the impression of people suffering a variety of illnesses and deficiencies and being subject to frequent physical traumas. These burials include a possible case of tuberculosis.[18] As remarked above however none of these burials was provided with grave goods, and most seem to have been buried with no great care; they may represent a particular and disadvantaged class in society, and should not necessarily be taken as indicative of the population as a whole. The cremation burials tend to be better provided with grave goods, while some, particularly the Folly Lane burial, demonstrate considerable wealth. This impression of a highly stratified society is confirmed by the differences in wealth apparent between the occupation sites at Gorhambury and Prae Wood (see above p40).

For all the warlike nature ascribed to the pre-Roman tribes of Britain by classical writers such as Caesar and Tacitus, there is little sign of a particularly 'military' lifestyle among the inhabitants of Verlamion. The massive dykes appear to have been constructed more for prestige than defence, while finds such as the fine enamelled linch pin from Kings Langley and the evidence for the production of elaborate linch pins found recently at Wheathampstead[19] are as likely to have decorated carts or wagons as to embellish war chariots. Ian Stead, the excavator of the King Harry Lane cemetery remarked on the complete absence of weapons from graves in Verulamium. This however may be due to ritual customs. It may well have been thought inappropriate to bury weapons in graves. Instead they may have been handed down to the next generation of warriors, or as Roymans has suggested, it is quite possible than when the time came for a warrior to retire, he would deposit his weapons as a votive offering, either at a site like Essenden, or in a river or marsh.[20]

With the exception of a possible warrior elite, the main preoccupation of the bulk of the inhabitants of Verlamion must have lain in agriculture. Cereal crops were clearly grown but environmental evidence has demonstrated the importance of pastoral farming in the area,[21] a finding borne out by Caesar's reference to the large number of cattle and (by implication from the 4000 chariots he claimed to have encountered) horses in the area.[22] The evidence of animal bones from the farmstead that pre-dated the Folly Lane burial site suggests that sheep also formed an important element in the pastoral economy, and a similar conclusion was reached from the analysis of animal bones from Gorhambury.[23] At King Harry Lane pork joints were the commonest food provided as grave offerings, but this may reflect a specifically funerary tradition.

Particularly important in the half century before the Roman conquest was the exploitation of the extensive deposits of bog iron in the upper Bulbourne valley 14km west of Verlamion (**16**). The main focus of the iron working was the site at Cow Roast, on Akeman Street 2km west of Berkhamsted. At its zenith in the first century AD the Cow Roast site covered an area of about 40ha and must have represented an extremely important economic resource. Verlamion, on the edge of the plateau overlooking the boulder clays of the Vale of St Albans, and commanding a natural crossing across the marshy Ver valley, was in an ideal position to control a trade route between Cow Roast and the rich areas of north-east Hertfordshire and north Essex. Certainly at the start of the Roman period it was this north-east/south-west axis through the town that was the most important route (**31**). An elite group based in Verlamion and able to control this trade would have been in an ideal position to exploit the newly opened Gallic markets. As much as anything else it may have been its favourable position in relation to the Cow Roast iron deposits that accounted for the dramatic rise of the Verlamion *oppidum* at the beginning of the first century AD.

Verlamion — documentary evidence and archaeological remains

No account of early Verulamium can ignore the growing number of references by classical writers to Britain, and which on occasion refer to named individuals. The earliest relevant historical reference to the area is to be found in Caesar's account of his campaign of 54 BC.[24] By the late summer of this year he had pushed north of the Thames, and was probably operating somewhere in the Lea valley. The native resistance was coordinated by an overall leader, Cassivellaunus whose base, described by Caesar as being defended by woods and marshes was presumably somewhere in the upper Lea. It must also have been defended by earthworks, or at least palisades, as large numbers of cattle had been driven into it for safety. Caesar evidently experienced some difficulty in finding this stronghold, and in the meantime was constantly harried by the guerrilla tactics of Cassivellaunus' forces. It was only with the help of a deputation from the Trinovantes of Essex and south Suffolk, long-standing enemies of Cassivelluanus, that he was finally able to reach it and crush the British resistance. Modern scholars also have difficulty in locating Cassivellaunus' stronghold. The Wheelers favoured Wheathampstead, 7.5km north of Verulamium, on the south side of the upper Lea valley. Here the Devils Dyke, a massive earthwork consisting of a ditch with banks on both sides, cut across a narrow neck of higher ground between the Lea valley and a dry valley to the south (**17, colour plate 3**). It is still an extremely impressive earthwork today; including both banks it has an overall width of 54m, and even in its present silted up state in places the ditch is 10m deep. Approximately 550m east of the Devils Dyke are the less well-defined earthworks known as the Moat and Slad. The Moat has clearly been adapted, probably in the post-medieval period, to provide ponds and field boundaries. Further north the Slad has been seen by some to be a purely natural feature, while others suggest it represents a natural gully that has been deliberately enlarged in the past to form the east side of the Iron Age enclosure. Today both the Moat and the Slad lie in a private estate, and in the absence of any excavation or detailed fieldwork it is impossible to be certain as to their original form, although casual inspection on the ground suggests to the writer that the Slad may well be a natural feature that has been deliberately adapted. At what date this took place remains unknown, but the plan, and the very marked way in which the Wheathampstead earthwork can be seen to enclose a specific area straddling the neck of high ground, suggests that the Slad, Moat and Devils Dyke all formed part of the same complex.

None of the Wheathampstead earthworks have been securely dated. The limited excavations that have been carried out here were those of the Wheelers in the early 1930s[25] but they recovered little evidence with which to date the earthworks. A la Tène II brooch, dating to about the mid-first century BC, was found in secondary context in the silt of the Devils Dyke, and pottery of a similar date was recovered from a small gully between the Dyke and the Slad. While these finds suggest a degree of occupation here at about the time of Caesar's campaign, it is still not certain that the earthworks were in existence by then; the brooch could well have been old by the time it came to be discarded in the ditch.

In view of all these uncertainties it would be unwise to postulate Wheathampstead as the site of Cassivellaunus' stronghold. There are other sites with at least as good a claim. One such site is Gatesbury, immediately south-east of Braughing, where undated, but apparently late Iron Age, earthworks defend a site which has produced significant quantities of pottery dating from the mid-first century BC.[26] Other possible sites lie further north-west on the Chiltern scarp such as the large hill fort at Ravensburgh in north Hertfordshire or even the *oppidum* at Baldock. What is certain is that there is no evidence to suggest that there was a Caesarian stronghold in the immediate vicinity of Verlamion, or indeed anywhere in the Ver valley. The Aubreys fort has produced no material of this, or any other date, and it is more likely to date from a significantly earlier phase of the Iron Age.

At the time of the Roman conquest Verlamion lay in the tribal territory of the Catuvellauni, who at the time were the dominant tribe in southern Britain. The similarity of the names has sometimes led to speculation that Cassivellaunus was a Catuvellaunian leader. There is no supporting evidence for this. Furthermore, the name Catuvellauni probably meant 'expert fighters'. Cassivellaunus on the other hand means 'outstanding', or 'handsome', and was an element in many names. The similarity between the two names is therefore probably coincidental and the interest of Caesar's account lies in its suggestion of a social pattern based on a number of small tribal units. In addition to the Trinovantes Caesar mentioned five tribal groups; two, the Cenimagni and the Segontiaci, are thought to have been based in Norfolk and Berkshire respectively, but the remaining three, the Ancalites, the Bibroci and the Cassi, may well have occupied territories in the Chilterns and the Colne and Lea valleys. In times of crisis these groups were clearly capable of operating together under a paramount leader.

Caesar left Britain in 54, and was never to return. To what extent south-eastern England was considered conquered is a matter of debate. Certainly Caesar himself claimed to have conquered Britain, making it, like Gaul, subject to the Roman *imperium.* Whether this view was shared by the British themselves is more debatable. Before leaving however, Caesar concluded treaties giving the Trinovantes Roman protection, and forcing Cassivellaunus to undertake not to attack them; in addition tribute had to be paid to Rome. As was Caesar's normal practice he also took hostages. It is somewhat doubtful, however, that the treaty was strictly observed for very long. The political situation in Italy, Caesar's murder in 44 BC and the ensuing civil war, meant that the newly conquered areas of Gaul were left largely to their own devices, and presumably this was even more the case in Britain. It was not until 27 BC that Augustus felt his position to be sufficiently secure to allow him to turn his attention to Gaul and the task of incorporating the tribal areas conquered by Caesar into an organised, Roman provincial system. It was at this point that according to the Greek historian Dio, Augustus planned a military campaign in Britain.[27] In the event this invasion never took place and instead Augustus agreed fresh treaties with British tribal leaders;[28] by 24/23 BC Rome had apparently abandoned the idea of a fresh campaign in Britain. Augustus' treaties probably required the payment of tribute to Rome, and quite possibly also the sending of hostages, while the fact that it was necessary to arrange fresh treaties implies that any earlier ones made by Caesar had by now lapsed. Treaties were invariably considered to have terminated on the death of the rulers concerned, and the British chieftains of Caesar's day may well have been dead by 27 BC.

It is tempting to see the volume of imported tableware at Braughing in the last quarter of the first century BC, as evidence of the renewal of contact with Rome via northern and central Gaul following Augustus' treaty arrangements. If this was the case however it did not extend to the Verlamion area where settlements, if they existed, continued to be virtually aceramic, and new burial traditions continued to be resisted. It was not until shortly before 10 or 15 BC that the area saw the appearance on some sites of imported tableware.

The clearest evidence for links with the Roman world is, however, the increasing influence of Roman prototypes on the design of coins minted in Britain at the end of the first century BC. The appearance of named individuals on British coins, often including the title *rex* or *rigon*, has led to the construction of quasi-political histories for the 'royal dynasties' of the Catuvellauni and their neighbours south of the Thames, the Atrebates. Important in this context is the analysis by John Creighton of the influence of Roman styles on locally produced coins. This has shown that by the end of the first century BC changes in designs on some British coins not only kept pace with changes in Italy, but also emphasised the pre-eminent position of the ruler.[29] Creighton argues that this is due to Rome's policy of taking hostages whereby the sons of native aristocrats were educated in Gaul or in Rome itself. They might then serve as officers in auxiliary units of the Roman army before finally returning to their original communities. Such an arrangement was not uncommon in Rome's dealings with tribes on the border of the empire and ensured that aristocratic elites in these areas became highly 'Romanised' and developed strong personal and political links with aristocratic families in Rome.

It is possible to see the appearance of Continental influence in the Verlamion in the end of the first century BC as the first fruits of such a policy. Following Augustus' visit to Gaul in 27 BC, young sons of an aristocratic elite in the Verlamion area could have been sent to be educated in Rome, or with a pro-Roman tribe in Gaul. While it is important to guard against over-interpretation of archaeological data in terms of historically recorded events, it remains true that in the last decade of the first century BC, there is for the first time substantial evidence for contacts, either direct or indirect, between the Verlamion area and the Roman Empire. By 15 or 10 BC hostages taken in *c.*27 BC could have been in a position to return to their original communities after serving for a period in the Roman army. This is precisely the time when new pottery styles, burial rites, and above all locally produced, inscribed coins first make their appearance in the Verlamion region.

The earliest inscribed coins in the area are those of Tasciovanus, sometimes linked with otherwise unknown individuals, Andoco, Sego, Riis and Dias. Tasciovanus' coins first appear in about 10 BC and a significant proportion bear the mint mark Vir or Verlamio implying that Verlamion was already the pre-eminent local settlement (**colour plate 7a**). In spite of this however, none of Tasciovanus' earliest coins have as yet been found in the Verlamion area. Instead they concentrate around Braughing. This is not to say that Verlamion was not by this time a significant centre. As we have seen the Verlamion *oppidum* comprised a number of settlement sites over a wide area, and it may simply be a matter of chance that the areas of late first-century occupation have not yet been excavated; certainly the earliest burials in the King Harry Lane cemetery are contemporary with the earliest issues of Tasciovanus. An additional reason for the rarity of early issues in Verlamion may lie in the uses to which the early coins were put. While coins may have been produced at central, high-status sites, they need not necessarily have been lost or discarded there. Coins were frequently deposited at religious sites, and they are perhaps more likely to have been lost at markets or trading centres rather than on farmsteads and occupation sites. Finally it is possible that the name Verlamion applied to the whole tract of land between Verlamion and Wheathampstead, and that pre-eminent settlements within it shifted from time to time. The recent discovery of a slab mould from late Iron Age contexts at Mackerye End in the Lea valley 2.5km north-west of Wheathampstead reminds us how little is certain about the size, status or role of settlements here in the last century before the Roman conquest. A few of Tasciovanus' early coins have the mint mark 'Camu' suggesting that for a brief period early in his reign Tasciovanus also controlled the principal Trinovantian centre, at Camulodunum (Colchester).

Whatever the status of Verlamion the coins of Tasciovanus mark an end to the differences in coin distribution patterns north and south of the upper Lea. This, combined with the spread of cremation burial, rectilinear enclosures and wheel-turned, grog-tempered pottery right across the Chiltern dip slope marks an end of the division apparent in the earlier first century BC, and presumably marks the beginning of the tribal ascendancy of the historically attested tribe of the Catuvellauni. Whether the Catuvellauni originated north or south of the upper Lea is another matter and one that at the moment is impossible to resolve, and very probably always will be. What is apparent is a shift in outlook in the area. We can only speculate as to whether this was because the Verlamion area was taken over by people originally based north of the Lea, or whether the rulers of a tribe centred in the Ver valley decided to adopt Roman ideas and imports and expand into neighbouring territories.

In *c.*AD 10 the coins of Tasciovanus were replaced by those of Cunobelin. Cunobelin describes himself on some issues as the son of Tasciovanus, although this may mean little more than successor to, or supplanter of, the previous ruler. Like Tasciovanus, Cunobelin included the mintmark Ver or Verul on some of his coins. His earliest issues however bear the Camulodunum mint mark and it is generally assumed that on succeeding Tasciovanus, Cunobelin immediately established himself at Camulodunum, creating a Catuvellaunian/Trinovantian confederacy that was to last until the Roman conquest. Throughout his long reign Cunobelin steadily extended his 'sphere of influence' to cover most of south-east England and the south Midlands. By the time of his death in about AD 40, the Roman historian Tacitus could describe him as king of the Britons.

Although eclipsed to some extent by Camulodunum, Verulamium continued to be a major centre throughout Cunobelin's reign. It is probable that it is to this period to which the majority of the slab moulds found at Verlamion belong. At the time of writing the quantities of imported material do not suggest as wealthy a population in Verlamion as that in Camulodunum. This again however may simply reflect the type of sites that have been excavated here. The largest quantity of material is that from the King Harry Lane cemetery. Here the 455 excavated cremation burials yielded over 700 pottery vessels. The bulk of these were locally made jars and platters, and while many imitated imported tableware, actual imported vessels formed less than 20% of the total. A similar picture was arrived at by Isobel Thompson in her study of the pre-Roman pottery excavated by the Wheelers at Prae Wood. This gave a picture in marked contrast to the situation at Sheepen (part of the Camulodunum *oppidum*) and Braughing where there were enormous quantities of imported pottery. The Folly Lane funerary shaft, however, contained more samian vessels imported from the south of France than the combined total of samian ware from the whole of the King Harry Lane cemetery, while the high-status occupation site at Gorhambury produced a significantly greater quantity of imported goods than Prae Wood. All this provides a vivid illustration of how luxury goods were monopolised by aristocratic elites. It may only be a matter of time before further high-status sites are discovered at Verlamion making it more comparable to Camulodunum. The history of Verulamium in the years after the Roman conquest is itself an indication of the continued importance of Verlamion in the final years of Cunobelin's rule, and in those of his successors.

3 The Roman town
The first 100 years

The Catuvellauni and the Roman Conquest

There are signs that as Cunobelin aged, feuds broke out among his sons. In AD 40 one son, Adminius, was forced to flee abroad and to appeal to the emperor Caligula for help. The Catuvellauni/Trinovantian confederacy however continued to be the most powerful group in the south-east. The Dobunni of the Cotswolds were described by Dio as being their clients and in AD 41 it was the threat of Catuvellaunian expansion south of the Thames that led Verica, the ruler of the Atrebates in Hampshire, to seek the protection of the emperor Claudius, thereby giving Rome a pretext for invasion in 43. Verica's flight was not the sole reason however. Raids on the Gallic coast and the demands of Cunobelin's sons, that Rome return at least two further rebels, must have made it clear that treaty arrangements of the sort that had held good throughout Cunobelin's reign were no longer effective. In any case the death of Cunobelin in about AD 40 would, in Roman eyes, have terminated any existing treaty. A decision to invade was taken by Caligula in 41, but abandoned at the last minute for reasons that are not entirely clear. Two years later the newly established emperor Claudius, who owed his position to the good will of the Praetorian guard and so was anxious to establish a military reputation with the army, launched the invasion.

Our main historical sources for the Claudian invasion are short accounts by the second-century writer Suetonius and the third-century historian Cassius Dio. Dio tells us that the invasion army, commanded by Aulus Plautius, sailed in three divisions. The conventional view of the course of events has been that all three divisions landed in Kent, establishing a base at the natural harbour at Richborough. The discovery of early military remains at Fishbourne, near Chichester, however, has led to a re-examination of this 'traditional' view and the suggestion that some or all of the invasion force landed on the south coast in the southern part of the Atrebates tribal area.[1] The Atrebates were clearly supporters of Rome; it was the appeal by Verica that had prompted the invasion in the first place, and it would have made sense for one section of the invading force to land in an area where loyalty to Rome could be relied on. Since the Atrebates controlled territory stretching from west Sussex to the Thames, this would also allow the Romans a safe passage north, via Silchester, to the Catuvellaunian territory in the Thames valley. A Roman force taking this route could have crossed the Thames in the region of Staines before pushing north into the heart of Catuvellaunian territory in Hertfordshire and Essex (**16** inset). The reinterpretation of the documentary sources, however, relies heavily on the early material from Fishbourne (which could have arrived there in the course of trade), so arguments as to the site of the initial landings and the lines of the subsequent advance continue. From the Verulamium perspective, they are not particularly relevant. Whether the landings took place in Kent or Sussex, or in both, the defeat of the Catuvellaunian/Trinovantian confederacy must have been the prime objective, and the attitude towards Rome of the section of the Catuvellauni in the south-west Chilterns would have been an important factor. Dio makes it clear that the Roman invasion was fiercely resisted by at least two of Cunobelin's sons, Caratacus and Togodumnus. Shortly after the invasion force had landed, both were defeated by Plautius in a pitched battle at a river crossing. Assuming that all three divisions of the Roman army had landed in Kent, this battle is usually thought to have taken place somewhere on the river Medway; a Sussex landing would mean the battle being fought somewhere on the river Arun. In any event, following this defeat, the combined Catuvellaunian and Trinovantian forces retreated north and the Roman army advanced to the Thames. Some of the Roman forces crossed the Thames by swimming, while others (probably the bulk of the army) crossed by bridge some distance further upstream. There were evidently further skirmishes in the marshes north of the Thames, and the death of Togodumnus at about this time may have hardened British resistance. At this point the emperor arrived in Britain with reinforcements, and Caratacus and the Catuvellaunian/Trinovantian confederacy were finally crushed. In what must by now have been the late summer, Claudius led his forces in person into Cunobelin's former capital at Camulodunum.

A territory covering as wide an area as that controlled by Cunobelin must have included numerous sub-groups, groups that no doubt included different and disparate factions. It is not difficult to imagine old rivalries between these groups persisting, only to surface as overall control weakened after Cunobelin's death. The differences in the settlement pattern that had existed little more than half a century earlier (discussed in the previous chapter), may have resulted in sub-groups forming in our area. While both Caratacus and Togodumnus must have controlled sufficiently extensive areas to be able to mobilise effective resistance to Rome, there may well have been sections within the Catuvellaunian/Trinovantian confederacy that did not share their fiercely anti-Roman stance. Traditional tribal rivalries and feuds among the aristocratic elite could have led a Catuvellaunian sub-group, perhaps based in the south-west Chilterns, to be inclined to assist, or at least not actively oppose, the Roman invasion. There is growing evidence to suggest that the section of the Catuvellauni around Verlamion was favourably treated by the Roman administration in the years following the conquest. This is particularly striking if early Roman Verulamium is compared to Camulodunum in the same period. At Camulodunum a legionary fortress was established immediately after the conquest, to be succeeded a few years later by a *colonia* of retired legionaries who exploited the native population and confiscated their land.[2] By contrast at Verulamium there is little or no sign of a phase of military occupation (as will be discussed below), but there is convincing evidence that the native aristocracy at least retained much of its wealth and social prestige. The obvious explanation for this very marked difference in treatment by the Romans is that the fiercely anti-Roman attitude of the population around Camulodunum was not shared in the Verlamion area. It is quite possible that the preferential treatment that

23 A selection of lead sling-shots collected during field walking south-west of Verulamium. Copyright St Albans Museum

Verlamion seems to have received in the post-conquest period was a reward for maintaining a neutral position on the Roman flank as it pushed north-east towards Camulodunum. This would have been particularly beneficial to any Roman force advancing into Essex from Berkshire, following an initial landing on the south coast.

Following the defeat of Caratacus in Essex, Dio tells us that Claudius either defeated or arranged treaties with many other tribes, a statement that is corroborated by two fragmentary inscriptions on a monumental arch in Rome recording the submission of British kings.[3] These chieftains may well have included leaders of smaller tribal sub-groups, one of which could have been that of the Verlamion Catuvellauni.

In the Verlamion region a particularly interesting site has been identified near Windridge, approximately 1km south-west of the Roman town (**19**). The site lies on the line of the road that linked Roman Verulamium with Akeman Street and beyond that with the Thames and the Atrebatic centre at Silchester. The route was presumably already in existence in the pre-conquest period. In the early 1980s a field-walking survey in the Windridge area recorded pottery dating from the mid-first to third centuries AD and suggesting an occupation site here. In addition at least 100 lead sling-shots have been found in the same area as well as British and early Roman coins, a lynch pin and small strap ends of first-century type.[4] The lead sling-shots (**23**) were of a type used by auxiliary units in the Roman army in the first century, and while it is possible that they derive from a small Roman fort, or even were manufactured on the site (metalworking debris has been recorded in the same fields) it is perhaps more likely that they mark the site of a skirmish, or even of a battle. It may be that an occupation site lies in this area, and that this was the scene of fighting some time in the mid-first century. To what extent (if at all) this involved the local population is unknown. It could have involved a group retreating towards Camulodunum after a defeat in the Thames valley, or supporters of Caratacus pushing west after the Roman occupation of Camulodunum. Nor can we automatically assume that the material derives from an incident in the course of the conquest; it could equally well have taken place 17 years later at the time of the Boudiccan revolt.

While the significance of the Windridge finds remains uncertain there are strong indications that a substantial section of the local population, or at any rate their leaders, were decidedly pro-Roman in their sympathies. There are two strands of evidence to support this suggestion; first is the absence of a conquest period fort at Verulamium, and second is the continuing wealth and prestige of the ruling native elite itself, for at least a decade after 43.

Verulamium in the conquest period

In the early 1960s Sheppard Frere argued for the presence of a Roman fort, established in 43 in the heart of what was to become the Roman town and presumably used to garrison the area and quell local resistance.[5] Two factors supported his arguments. The first was the course of Watling Street. In the southern part of Roman Verulamium Watling Street, the main road between Verulamium and London, follows a diagonal course, cutting across the normal street grid of the town. It was reasonable to suggest that this was due to the presence of an early fort, established before the town street grid was laid out, and lying somewhere between the river and the area later occupied by the Roman Forum and Basilica. What seemed to be strong supporting evidence was provided by the discovery in 1956 of a bank, over 3m wide and faced with cut turf. Both faces of the bank had also been reveted with horizontally laid logs, supported by wooden uprights. The bank overlay the remains of an earlier workshop with several fragments of clay slab moulds; it also sealed a *dupondius* of Claudius, proving that it cannot have been constructed earlier than AD 41, the year in which Claudius became emperor.

A few years after the discovery of the bank the staff of the Verulamium museum excavated an entrance through it, generally referred to as the 'Timber Tower' and interpreted as the gateway into the fort from the north-east.[6]

Together these two pieces of pieces of evidence made a strong case for the presence of a fort somewhere in insulae XVII and XIX of the later town; consequently throughout the 1970s and 1980s Verulamium was frequently cited as a town which had developed from a short-lived, conquest period fort. In the course of the 1980s however evidence gradually accumulated which could not easily be fitted into this model of Verulamium's early history. Although clearly dating from after the Roman conquest, the plan of the 'Timber Tower' did not conform to those of Roman fort gates. The remains are now interpreted as those of a brushwood causeway leading across the marshy valley floor (see below) and supported by timber piles. Nor were any specifically military structures such as barrack blocks found in excavations within the area of the supposed fort. The comparatively small numbers of Claudian coins recorded from the town posed another problem. Following the conquest, large quantities of Roman bronze coinage appeared in the country in the wake of the Roman army. Roman soldiers were paid in gold but needed to exchange this for lower value bronze coins for routine transactions, yet in Verulamium there are far too few Claudian coins of any denomination to support the idea of a significant military occupation here.[7]

It was a clearer understanding of the early course of Watling Street however that cast most doubt on the existence of a conquest period fort at Verulamium. Between 1986 and

24 *A Roman bronze*
   helmet from
   Verulamium.
   Copyright St
   Albans Museum

1988 excavations south of the Forum showed that even in its earliest form Watling Street had never cut diagonally across central Verulamium.[8] Consequently, unless there was a fort somewhere at the southern end of the later town, an area that has produced no supporting evidence, some other reason has to be found to explain the street's course. In fact, as will be suggested later, the diagonal length of Watling Street was not laid out until the '70s or '80s, by which time it was aiming, not for a fort, but for the Roman town itself.

While there is little evidence to suggest a fort beneath Verulamium, there remains the possibility that there was a short-lived fort somewhere else in the area, either in the conquest period or in the years after the Boudiccan revolt. The possibility that the slingshots south of Verulamium mark the site of a small fort has already been mentioned. Another possible fort site lies on the raised land immediately north-east of the Ver at Kingsbury. The site overlooks the Ver crossing, and although covering only about 2ha and restricted on the north and east by a dry valley, it could have accommodated a small auxiliary unit. In 1982 a medieval field ditch running along the southern and eastern edges of the area was found to have cut into another, earlier ditch, possibly dating from the Roman period. A small amount of rather later Roman pottery has also been recorded from the area, although this probably relates to its use as a cemetery in the late second and third centuries.

Although there is still no firm evidence for the existence of a Roman fort at Verulamium there remains the problem posed by the quantity of Roman 'military equipment' found in and around the town. Indeed, with two *loricae*, a complete helmet and over 30 smaller items such as fragments of shield binding, decorative pendants of the type used by Roman cavalry units, chapes, and 'military' belt and cuirass mounts, the Verulamium Museum contains an impressive collection of Roman military equipment (**24-6**). Many of the small items were found in metalworking contexts and may simply be

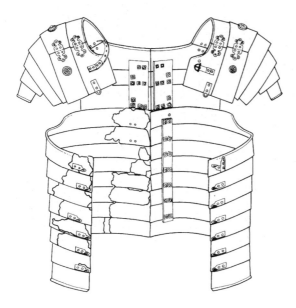

25 Part of an iron lorica found in a mid-first-century pit in Verulam Hills Field. Drawn by Philip Dean

scrap material awaiting reuse. Two items in particular, however, are more difficult to explain in these terms. One is the fine, early Roman helmet, stamped with the owner's name, Papirus and found, supposedly in Verulamium, in the last century. Its exceptionally good preservation suggests it may have been deposited in the marsh or river as a votive offering, and thus protected for nearly 2000 years by layers of peat or alluvium. Ritual deposition may also explain the preservation of another piece of armour. In 1966 a large fragment of a *lorica segmentata* was found in a small pit, dug sometime in the second half of the first century AD just outside the Roman town. About a quarter of the *lorica* survived; the leather straps connecting the iron hoops had been carefully cut, the hoops themselves had been neatly concertinaed together and the whole thing placed in the base of the pit. The pit was sited in the corner of a ditched funerary enclosure at Verulam Hills Field (**25**). The care with which the *lorica* had been quartered and buried, and its presence within the funerary enclosure, hints very strongly at a ritual deposition. It may not be going beyond the evidence to suggest that the other three (unexcavated) corners of the funerary enclosure accommodated the remaining three-quarters of the *lorica*, thus affording the enclosure a symbolic protection.

It is clear therefore that while the military equipment from Verulamium certainly suggests the presence of Roman soldiers, these were not necessarily serving soldiers garrisoned in the town. Along the middle and lower Rhine frontier in particular, there is a considerable body of evidence for the deposition of military equipment both in rivers and in native cult sites during the first century AD. This material has been seen as belonging to native veterans from auxiliary units in the Roman army, who, after their discharge, returned home and dedicated part of their equipment to the local deity.[9] The local Catuvellauni may well have observed similar traditions.

The occasional occurrence of very similar fittings from occupation sites at Park Street and Gorhambury, both of which developed into Roman villas in the later first century, suggests that local warriors were recruited into the army, either in the conquest period or in the years leading up to it. It is the Folly Lane burial however that provides the most dramatic evidence in this respect.

26 A complete iron mail tunic from the mid-first-century 'chieftain's burial' at Folly Lane. Copyright St Albans Museum

The Folly Lane burial

Mention has already been made of this burial (above p46). Among the rich collection of pyre goods was a complete iron mail *lorica* (**26-7**) and fragments of harness mounts of the type used by first-century cavalry units in the Roman army.[10] Yet the elaborate rite that evidently preceded the burial shows that it was firmly rooted in native, aristocratic tradition. The burial's remarkable wealth, the size of the funerary enclosure and the complexity of the associated rites all justify its description as a royal grave while its position, on the skyline overlooking the area that was to become the Roman town centre, seems expressly designed to ensure that the person buried here continued to dominate the local community in death, as he had done in his life. The samian ware found in the funerary shaft however dates from the mid 50s of the first century AD, at least ten years after the Roman conquest, while some of the pyre goods, notably the harness fittings, imply it was the grave of someone who had served as a cavalry officer in an auxiliary unit in the Roman army. In fact the Folly Lane burial provides a vivid demonstration of the Roman policy of using the native elite as the agent for the dissemination of *'Romanitas'* or the 'Romanisation' of native communities. As a member of this elite group, it is possible that his first experience of Roman culture was as a hostage. As mentioned above, boys from aristocratic native families who were sent as hostages could well go on to serve as auxiliary officers in the Roman army. As an officer in an auxiliary unit, his experiences would have covered far more than purely military matters. He would have travelled along engineered roads, staying in *mansiones* (the official guesthouses maintained for Roman officials); he would have been familiar with Roman baths, diet and a full monetary economy; he would have participated in the numerous religious rites and ceremonies, many of them expressly designed to foster loyalty to the emperor, that peppered the Roman year; and he would have been accustomed to seeing administration and justice dispensed in the *principia* (headquarters) of Roman forts or in the *fora* of provincial towns.

As has already been pointed out, the attitude of the population of the south-west Chilterns and Lea valley would have been crucial to any detachment of the Roman army

27 *A lathe-turned, ornamental knob (3.2cm high) made of elephant ivory, probably from a chair or couch. Found in the Folly Lane burial. The coloration is due to the partial burning of the object in the funeral pyre.* Copyright St Albans Museum

advancing into Essex after crossing the Thames west of London. The same concerns would apply equally in the case of subsequent advances after 43, west along the line along Stane Street and Akeman Street. The Folly Lane burial suggests there was an element among the native elite locally that could be relied upon to cooperate, controlled by a powerful individual who had seen service in the Roman army. Whether he was a client king (implying a formal treaty arrangement with Rome) or a *princeps civium* (chief citizen) is impossible to say, but we can safely assume that he was a man who had displayed sufficient pro-Roman sympathies at the time of the conquest to allow him to retain his wealth and position for over a decade after the conquest.

The earliest Roman town

Whatever the exact status of the man buried at Folly Lane may have been, his burial was conducted with all the traditional ceremonies a good ten years after the conquest. In fact there is little evidence from the Verulamium area as a whole for disruption at the time of the conquest. Indeed, as far as Verulamium is concerned were it not for references in classical texts, we might not realise that Claudius conquered the area at all. As the excavator of the King Harry Lane cemetery remarked, 'Britons in the south-east of England fought, were defeated, and conquered. These dramatic events had no effect on the funerary ritual at King Harry Lane, but the alien impinged on the cemetery about a generation later.'[11]

The absence of disruption however, does not mean that Verulamium stagnated in the 40s and early 50s. One of the most pronounced features of this period was a shift in the pattern of settlement away from the plateau edge to the lower valley slope, where it centred around the site occupied by the Central Enclosure beneath the later Forum/Basilica complex. In the early first century, access to the valley floor had clearly been restricted, either for religious reasons, or because it was reserved for a 'royal' estate.

At all events, the cross-country linear ditches prevented easy access from the plateau top, and entrances into the 'farmstead enclosures' were invariably on the south, east or west sides. In the mid-first century all this changed. The changes at Gorhambury provide a typical example. During the first two phases of late Iron Age occupation here, access to the site followed the normal practice and was restricted to the southern and western sides of the enclosures. It was only in the final phase that the New Dyke was deliberately laid out to allow direct access between Gorhambury and the valley floor. As was remarked in the previous chapter, however, this did not take place until the conquest period, and may well actually post-date the invasion. It was not until the third quarter of the first century that secondary causeways were laid across the Folly Lane ditch and the Wheeler ditch (at the corner of Pond Field), while the crossing across the same ditch in the King Harry Lane cemetery was made at a later date still.

In the early first century AD the cross-country route between Cow Roast and Welwyn and Colchester must have been of major importance (**16**). Where this route had crossed the river Ver in the early first century AD is uncertain but if the main function of the Beech Bottom dyke and Devils ditch was to define a cross-country route, the pre-Roman crossing point presumably lay about a kilometre upstream of the Roman crossing (**17**). At about the time of the Roman conquest however a river crossing was established close to the area that was to become the Roman town centre and directly opposite the new entrances through the Folly Lane ditch and the Wheeler ditch (**34a**). This river crossing lay on the site of the entrance through the Claudian turf and timber bank — the so-called 'Timber Tower'. The problems of reconciling the plan of the wooden uprights found here with the remains of a military gateway have already been mentioned. Photographs taken during the 1967 excavations however strongly suggest that while some of the 'Timber Tower' uprights no doubt revetted the ends of the turf and timber bank on either side of it, others were simply piles supporting a brushwood causeway across the marsh (**28**). In the later first century a metalled surface was laid over the brushwood causeway, and this continued to carry the road out of Verulamium and across the marsh until the mid-second century. Nevertheless, its relationship to the turf and timber bank and material found lodged between the piles and brushwood show that it must date initially to the mid-first century AD.

This opening up of access to the lower slopes and valley floor was mirrored by a gradual abandonment of many settlement sites on the plateau edge. In the absence of excavation it is impossible to trace this process in detail, but pottery collected from field walking suggests that sites at Parkbury, Oaklands, Beaumont Avenue, Beaumont Hall Farm, Harpenden Golf Course, Redbourn and Kinsbourne Green were all abandoned between about AD 60 and 100. It was only on sites that later developed into villas (Park Street, Gorhambury, Mackerye End, Woodcock Hill and probably Childwickbury) that occupation continued.

The construction of the 'Timber Tower' causeway was almost certainly contemporary with an expansion of the Central Enclosure. What must represent a northern extension to it was found during excavations beneath the new entrance to the Verulamium Museum in 1998.[12] The site lies immediately north-east of the Central Enclosure and the excavations revealed the top of a substantial ditch, approximately 3m wide at its mouth and more than

28 The surface of the mid-first-century brushwood track at the 'Timber Tower' during excavation in 1966. Copyright St Albans Museum

a metre deep, and although its true depth and initial date are still unknown, it is clear that it was not filled in before *c.*75, a generation after the Roman conquest. Earlier work in the area suggested that this ditch had run north-east along the west side of what was to be insula XVIII of the Roman town. Two separate excavations in 1961 recorded a substantial cut, at least 2m deep, into the natural subsoil beneath the street between insulae XVIII and XIX in 1960 and 1961.[13] Although the contemporary turf and timber bank along the northern sides of insulae XIX and XVII is probably part of the same circuit, the full extent of these mid-first-century earthworks is obscure. One possible circuit however is shown on figure **29**, where it is suggested that a substantial ditch, excavated in 1935 by Kathleen Kenyon under the north-west edge of the theatre, represents a further continuation. This would make a large annexe on the northern and western sides of the Central Enclosure.

The only buildings of this date for which reasonably complete plans are available are those of a range of workshops along the north-east side of insula XIV of the later town. They stood within the area of the annexe and were excavated by Sheppard Frere between 1955 and 1961 and interpreted as a single block put up soon after the conquest.[14] It is certainly possible to reconstruct the building as a block of at least ten rooms, 6m wide, sharing a common roof and opening onto the street through a shared portico or colonnade; to the rear of the main rooms additional lean-tos and extensions of differing dimensions were built (**30**). Frere suggested the whole block had been built by a landowner or speculator and then either rented out or worked by slaves or freedmen. Several of the 'units' seem to have been used by metal smiths. Crucibles were found in association with a small oven in one of the front rooms, while two others had small tubs,

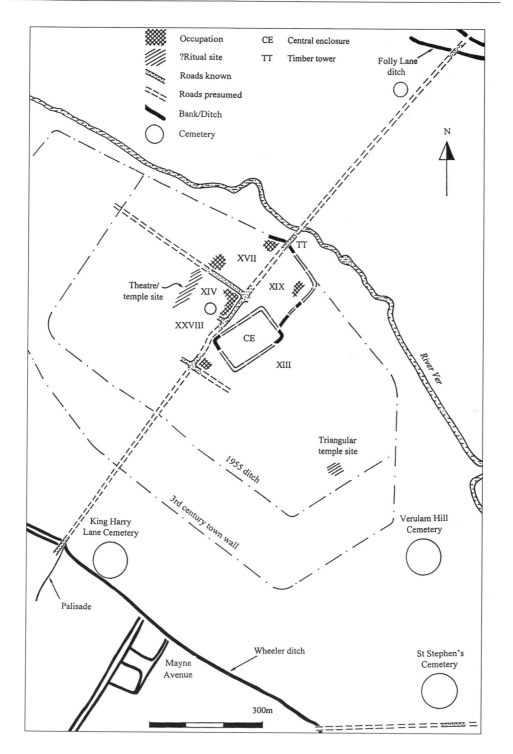

Occupation
CE   Central enclosure
?Ritual site
TT   Timber tower
Roads known
Roads presumed
Bank/Ditch
Cemetery

Folly Lane ditch

N

XVII

Theatre/ temple site

XIV

XIX

XXVIII

CE

XIII

River Ver

Triangular temple site

1955 ditch

3rd century town wall

King Harry Lane Cemetery

Verulam Hill Cemetery

Palisade

Wheeler ditch

Mayne Avenue

St Stephen's Cemetery

300m

29 Pre-Boudiccan Verulamium. Drawn by Terry Hunns

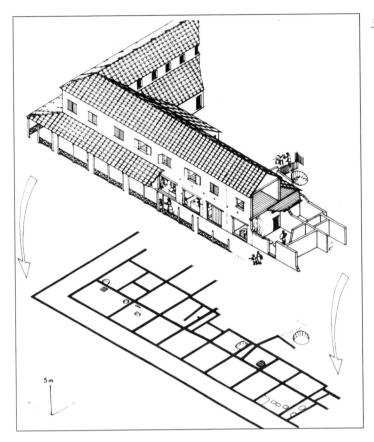

30 The workshops in insula XIV as they may have appeared shortly before the Boudiccan revolt. Drawn by Alex Thorne, after Frere

apparently placed beneath work-benches to collect shavings from bronze-workers' lathes. These front rooms may have been used as shops and workshops with living and storage quarters in the less regularly planned rooms at the rear. When necessary (for instance at night) the shops could be closed off from the colonnade by wooden shutters.

The whole block had been destroyed by fire, and the resulting layer of burnt debris contained much evidence of the building techniques employed. The workshops had rested on wooden cill beams supporting timber-framed superstructures, and the intervening spaces between the main uprights filled with lath and plaster. The absence of roof tiles suggested wooden or thatched roofs, and while most floors appear to have been of gravel or beaten clay, at least one room preserved traces of a planked floor. When the workshops were excavated it was thought that the use of cill beams in construction was an innovation introduced by the Roman army, so its use here was seen as additional evidence for a Roman military presence. It is now clear that this method of building was employed locally in the pre-Roman period, and indeed the sophistication of the cill beam construction and timber framing evident in the Folly Lane funerary structure suggests that local builders were adept at this type of construction. Nevertheless, the plan of the insula XIV block, with colonnade and multiple rooms under a single roof, is a totally new development. Small areas of timber-framed building resting on cill beams have also been recorded from below the *macellum* 100m north-west of the insula XIV block, and in the

1 An aerial view of Verulamium from the east. The band of trees (left centre) marks the line of the third-century town walls. The running track in the foreground lies in the former Verulam Hills Field, a short distance outside the London Gate of Verulamium. St Michaels Church, in the centre of the photograph, stands on the site of the Forum/Basilica, at the centre of the Roman town. Fishpool Street, bordering the traditional site of Kingsbury, is the curving street on the right hand side of the plate. Photo Charles Dobson

2 Reused Roman tile in the eleventh-century tower of the Cathedral and Abbey Church of St Alban. It is possible that the pillars also derive from the Roman town. Copyright St Albans Museum

3 The Devils Dyke, Wheathampstead. Photo Charles Dobson

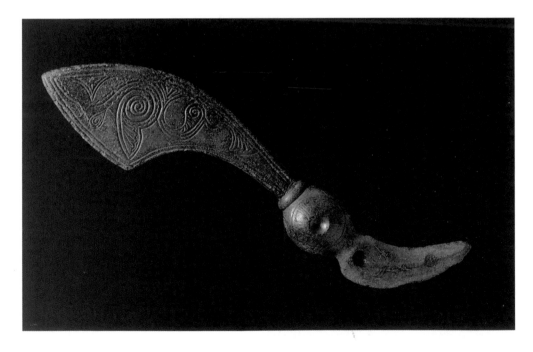

4 Small bronze knife, decorated with incised curvilinear designs. Found a short distance south of Verulamium. Overall length 11cm. Copyright, British Museum

5   *The Beech Bottom Dyke.* Photo Charles Dobson

6   *A well-preserved bridle bit and cheek piece, both decorated with enamel, from the mid-first-century 'chieftain's burial' at Folly Lane.* Copyright St Albans Museum

7   a. *Gold coin of Tasciovanus shown carrying a* carnyx *or war trumpet. Remains of what may have been a similar trumpet were found in the Folly Lane burial; b. gold coin of Cunobelin; c. reverse of a gold coin of Cunobelin, with the Verlamion mint mark.* Copyright St Albans Museum

8   *Fragments of mid-first-century painted wall plaster showing part of a lyre (left) and foliage (right). From the early bathhouse in insula XIX.* Copyright St Albans Museum

9   A rich collection of grave offerings in a late first-century burial on the northern edge of the King Harry Lane cemetery. The iron object in the background is the frame for a folding chair. The cremated ashes of an elderly individual were contained in the largest of the glass jars. Copyright St Albans Museum

10 *The central panel from one of the earliest mosaics from Verulamium showing an urn and two dolphins. From a house in insula XXVIII destroyed in the Antonine fire of c.155.* Copyright St Albans Museum

11 *Mid-second-century painted wall plaster from the same house as the dolphin mosaic (colour plate 10). This plaster was also a victim of the fire of c.155.* Copyright St Albans Museum

12 Burnt surfaces and cill beams in the building in the south corner of insula XIII (illustrated figure 46) destroyed in the fire of c.155. In the foreground is a chalk base (?for heavy equipment) with burnt posts, beams and a wooden tub set into it. Copyright St Albans Museum

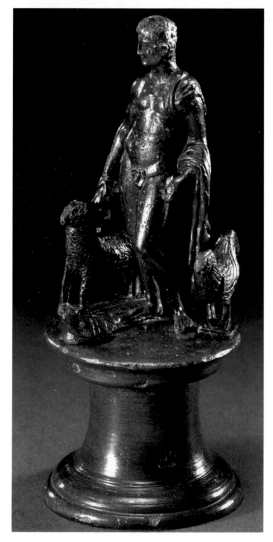

13 *A bronze* patera *or skillet, from water-*
logged deposits in the valley floor, immedi-
ately north-east of the 'Timber Tower'.
Maximum diameter 13.4cm. Copyright
St Albans Museum

14 *Bronze statuette of Mercury with a cocker-*
el, ram and tortoise, found in the filling of
a ditch on the east side of the King Harry
Lane cemetery. Overall height (including
plinth) c.63cm. Copyright St Albans
Museum

15 *Bronze statuette of Apollo from the King Harry Lane area. Overall height, c.8.8cm.* Copyright St Albans Museum

16 *Bronze statuette of Venus found in an early fourth-century cellar in insula XIV. Overall height c.20cm.* Copyright St Albans Museum

17 *The central panel from a later second-century mosaic from insula IV showing a horned god; he is either a water god with lobster claws around his head, or a woodland deity with animal horns.* Copyright St Albans Museum

18 *Painted plaster from the ceiling in a corridor in the late second-century building 2, insula XXI. Doves and panther (or leopard) masks are framed by ears of corn and flowers.* Copyright St Albans Museum

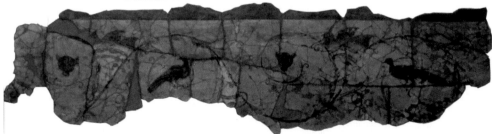

20 Painted wall plaster from a courtyard wall in building 2, insula XXI. British Copyright, British Museum

21 *The well-preserved late second-century mosaic floor from building 2, insula XXI, showing a lion carrying a stag's head. The dark patch on the floor was probably caused by a brazier scorching the floor. The room had no hearth or hypocaust.* Reproduced courtesy of the St Albans Museum, copyright reserved

22 An aerial photograph looking north-east across Watling Street as it runs across private land towards the Chester Gate. The foundations of a large house, apparently with its own apsidal bath suite, are clearly visible a short distance north of Watling Street which runs across the centre of the photograph. The outline of a large rectangular structure, with a T-shaped corridor, flanked by two large rooms and leading to a ?walled yard is visible lower right. The function of this building is unknown (p109). Copyright St Albans Museum

23 The projecting bastion at the south corner of the third-century town wall. Photograph Charles Dobson

24 The third-century town wall and beyond it, on the other side of the river Ver, the Cathedral and Abbey Church of St Alban. The lake is on the site of the fishpond that served the Abbey in the Middle Ages. Photograph Charles Dobson

25 Post holes for a post-Roman timber building on the Folly Lane/Oysterfield site. The building fronted onto a 'hollow way' that succeeded the Roman road leading north-east from Verulamium. On the photograph the hollow way can be seen as a band of dark earth. Copyright St Albans Museum south corner of insula XIV and the east corner of insula XXVIII. Unfortunately in neither case could complete plans be recovered and there is as yet nothing to tell us whether or not the insula XIV block was unique in the town.

An exception to the general run of early structures was a masonry building on the east side of insula XIX. It was found by Chris Saunders in a small rescue excavation in 1973, but only a very small part of it could be exposed. The building contained a sunken area, 1.1m deep, which had been lined with mortar and surrounded by a colonnade of oolitic limestone columns resting on a flint and mortar dwarf wall. The columns, together with fragments of painted wall plaster with designs including foliage and a lyre (**colour plate 8**) indicated considerable sophistication and the sunken area was interpreted as a plunge bath in a mid-first-century bathhouse. The bath building overlay pits and remains of a clay wall associated with grog-tempered pottery, and was dated to the pre-Boudiccan period on this basis. This dating is supported by flue tiles from the building which are of a distinctive 'thin-walled' variety, a type of tile that has been identified as being characteristic of the mid-first century.[15] The remains of burnt timbers, apparently from the roof, which were found lying on the floors, were interpreted as evidence of the destruction caused by the Boudiccan revolt. The explanation that the building was a bathhouse is certainly the most reasonable one but the evidence for its date is rather less secure. Grog-tempered pottery continued to be used at least until the third quarter of the first century, so it is conceivable that the building was not put up until shortly after the Boudiccan revolt, and that the burnt timber on the floor results from a later incident. Whatever caused the burning it did not result in the total destruction of the building which continued in use until the end of the first century.[16]

Another masonry building that may date to shortly after the conquest lies approximately 250m south-west of the bathhouse, beneath the later Forum. Here the excavations in the early 1900s revealed small lengths of flint and mortar walls, some of them bearing painted wall plaster, and in one area associated with a mortar floor. No plan or dating evidence was recovered but the walls clearly pre-dated the main Forum/Basilica complex (**35**). We shall come to the whole question of the date of the Forum/Basilica in a later section, but as far as these early walls are concerned there is a particular question that still has to be resolved: does the fragmentary inscription which commemorated the completion of the Forum/Basilica in AD 79 refer to a later building programme or does the inscription really relate to these earlier walls themselves?

For many years it has been thought that the street grid of Roman Verulamium was established, at least in the central area of the town, by the time of the Boudiccan revolt of AD 61. The reason for this was the way in which the Forum/Basilica complex at the centre of the town appeared to have been superimposed on a pre-existing street layout, with a resulting misfit between the Forum entrances and the streets on the south-west sides of insulae XIII and XXVIII.[17] The position of the Forum entrances, however, was based on work carried out by Bicknell and Page at the beginning of the twentieth century, when a mistake was made in measuring the positions of the small excavations dug from time to time in the vicarage garden and plotted from the (since demolished) Victorian vicarage. This mistake resulted in the entrances appearing on published plans approximately 12.5m too far to the south-west. If the original mistake is rectified, the mismatch between entrances and streets largely disappears, and with it the main argument for supposing a well-established, pre-Boudiccan street grid. Such streets as there were in the 40s and 50s were uncambered, gravelled tracks, usually without well-defined side ditches; it was not until the last quarter of the first century that properly metalled, cambered streets with timber lined drainage gullies on each side were laid out. In fact there is now little evidence to suggest that a regularly planned street grid was already in existence before the Boudiccan revolt. No doubt there was a tendency for lanes to develop more or less at right angles to the main through road leading to the 'Timber Tower' causeway, but there is little sign of consistency in the size of the blocks or *insulae* that these lanes defined.

Figure **29** shows the distribution within Verulamium of occupation sites which can be dated to the middle decades of the first century. This suggests a small settlement covering not more than 10-12ha (24-8 acres) and clustered along the south-west/north-east through road on the north-west side of the Central Enclosure, leading to the 'Timber Tower' causeway across the marsh in the valley floor. This is a far smaller settlement than was once thought to have existed here at the time of the Boudiccan revolt.[18] It may well have been contained within the boundaries of the Central Enclosure and its 'annexe' to the north. Yet in spite of its relatively small size, mid-first-century Verulamium appears to have been a place of considerable wealth, and one where Roman innovations were quickly adopted. It has already been suggested that the Central Enclosure, under what was to become the centre of the Roman town, was a 'special' area before the conquest, whether as a high-status occupation site, or as an industrial centre or religious focus, or as a combination of all three. In the early Roman period this 'special' status continued. Certainly wealth seems to have been concentrated in this area. When the southern arm of the Central Enclosure ditch was finally levelled in *c.*70 the levelling material contained exceptionally large quantities of samian and imported fine ware, while 150m to the west, one of the insula XIV 'workshops' contained a large collection of imported south-Gaulish samian ware.[19] This is in marked contrast to the pottery from the later graves in King Harry Lane cemetery and from most occupation sites in the hinterland of Verulamium which continued to be dominated by locally made grog-tempered wares, with little or no imported fine tableware, or even the products of the earliest 'Roman' kilns established in *c.*55, 3km south of Verulamium at Bricket Wood.[20] Here surely is a clear example of a local elite, based in what was to become the centre of the Roman town, patronising the metalworkers in the insula XIV workshops and monopolising the supply of imported tableware. This elite must also have been responsible for the two early masonry buildings in the area, the walls beneath the south-west side of the Forum and the insula XIX bathhouse.

The status of Verulamium at this stage in its history is uncertain. Tacitus, writing at the end of the century, describes Verulamium as a *municipium*. A *municipium* was a town with a charter granted by the emperor and giving certain, carefully defined privileges. These privileges varied, but in the first century it was a status granted only to settlements that had already achieved a certain degree of Romanisation. The wealth, the pro-Roman attitude of the Verulamium elite and the early appearance of Romanised buildings in insula XIX and the Forum support the suggestion that the town had already achieved municipal status in the Claudio/Neronian period. On the other hand, as will be seen below, it was not until the succeeding Flavian period, in *c.*75-85, that the town expanded and was demonstrably equipped with its full quota of public buildings. Tacitus could still have referred to the town as a *municipium*, even though the events he was describing — in this case the Boudiccan revolt — had taken place before this status was granted.

The Boudiccan Revolt

In AD 61 the tribes of Norfolk, Suffolk and Essex, the Iceni and Trinovantes, under the Icenian queen Boudicca, united in revolt against Rome. According to Tacitus, Verulamium was destroyed by the rebels along with London and Colchester before the revolt was crushed.

At Verulamium the death of the chieftain buried at Folly Lane had only recently occurred. The new Roman town was in the process of being built, but as yet, apart from workshops and stores, consisted of little more than a few 'luxury' buildings in and around the old Central Enclosure; even these may have been only half-built. Away from this aristocratic nucleus old ways continued unchanged. Most of the established farmsteads along the plateau edge remained unaltered; the gradual abandonment that affected many of them in the last quarter of the first century had not yet commenced. The traditional burial rites also continued unaltered, as no doubt did other 'rites of passage'. Against this background it is easy to envisage the persistence of tribal feuds and rivalries; in particular, resentments dating back to pro- and anti-Roman stances at the time of the conquest were probably still smouldering. This must be the reason why Verulamium suffered the same fate at the hands of the rebels as more 'Roman' settlements at Colchester and London. When the revolt first broke out the Roman governor, Suetonius Paulinus, was campaigning in north Wales with the bulk of the army. Although he had returned to London on hearing news of the revolt, the main body of the army did not arrive in time to save Verulamium. According to Tacitus, the rebels sacked the town; its buildings were presumably burnt and any inhabitants unwise enough to have remained there were massacred. It cannot have been long afterwards, however, that the final confrontation between Boudicca and the Romans took place, a confrontation that resulted in the defeat of the rebels and the death of Boudicca.

Documentary evidence for the Boudiccan revolt is provided by Tacitus and Dio. As far as Verulamium is concerned, archaeological evidence is less clear. Verulamium has not, so far, produced extensive evidence for contemporary burning comparable to that found at Colchester. At Verulamium the only buildings that were definitely destroyed at about this time were the workshops in insula XIV and the early timber buildings beneath the later *macellum* in insula XVII; the bathhouse in insula XIX may also have been damaged but it was not totally destroyed. Burnt deposits at low levels in excavations in other parts of the Roman town, most of them found in the 1930s, have since been shown to contain pottery made in kilns at Highgate Wood, north-west of London, and dating from not earlier than *c.*AD 80. All this confirms the impression that at the time of the revolt Verulamium was still very much an emerging town where there was, as yet, comparatively little to destroy in terms of 'Roman' buildings. Lack of excavation makes it difficult to gauge the effects on 'native' farmsteads in the immediate area, although on the sites that have seen excavation — Gorhambury, Park Street and Prae Wood — it is difficult to identify destruction layers that can be attributed to Boudicca with any degree of confidence.

31 The site of the early town. Prae Wood lies in private land in the wooded area on the skyline in the top left-hand corner; the edge of the gravel terrace on which the early town was sited can be clearly seen running across the centre of the photograph. Copyright St Albans Museum

The post-Boudiccan Town

The difficulty of identifying solid archaeological evidence in the form of destroyed buildings does not mean to say that the effects of the revolt on the local population were not disastrous. One of the few sites that has seen large-scale excavation in this period is that of the workshops in insula XIV. Not only were these totally destroyed in the revolt but it was some 15 years before they were rebuilt. In 61 Roman Verulamium was only just beginning to be established but its buildings were being planned on lavish lines; the aristocratic elite was indulging in exotic and expensive imports, and workshops were producing fine metalwork. Pre-Boudiccan Verulamium was a high-status settlement, quite possibly one that was being planned as a 'show town'. The time taken for confidence to be recovered is one indication of the severity of the blow caused by the Boudiccan destruction. In the aftermath of the revolt, those of the tribal elite who had survived may have decided it would be more prudent to use their wealth in safer ways than in ostentatious buildings that could be destroyed in a rising. The recently discovered hoard of 134 gold and silver coins dating from the Flavian period and found at Shillington, 27km north of Verulamium, is evidence of substantial wealth among the Chiltern Catuvellauni. This was wealth, however, that was hoarded, or in this case perhaps given as offerings at a shrine or temple; it was not used to pay for public display in the form of new houses.

The 15 years taken for the recovery of the insula XIV workshops may or may not prove typical of Verulamium as a whole; only further excavation will resolve this. Certainly, however, the next phase at Verulamium is characterised by the construction of what are best described as public works. The Neronian (54-68) and the Flavian (69-96) periods covered the half-century when Verulamium was established on the lines that were to govern the topography of St Albans for a thousand years.

Crucial to the development of post-Boudiccan Verulamium was the rise of London. In the pre-Roman period the main route for imports from the continent had been between the mouth of the Rhine and the Thames estuary and Essex coast. This must largely have accounted for the importance of Camulodunum at the end of the pre-Roman Iron Age.

32 An aerial view of the modern A5183 on the line of Roman Watling Street, 3km north-west of Verulamium. Copyright St Albans Museum

Most imported goods coming into pre-conquest Verlamion were probably carried across north Essex to Braughing, and then via Welwyn and Wheathampstead; some may also have come into the area from the south coast via Silchester and Staines. Alternative routes would have run along the Icknield Way from the middle Thames or the Wash, reaching Verulamium via the late Iron Age settlements at Dunstable or Cow Roast, or from the Thames via the rivers Lea and Colne. Compared to pre-Roman Chichester and Colchester, Verlamion was remote from principal sources of supply in terms of continental imports.

All this changed in the middle years of the first century AD, when London developed with astonishing speed, first into a major trading centre, and then into the provincial capital. London lies only 20 miles to the south-east of Verulamium; a day's march for a Roman army unit, and a day's journey for pack-horses and wagons. In the Roman period two major routes from London to the north and west diverged at Verulamium. Akeman Street led ultimately to Cirencester, Gloucester and south Wales. After leaving Verulamium it ran along the Gade valley, and followed the pre-Roman route that had linked Cow Roast with Verlamion. This route, continuing to Welwyn and Braughing to the north-east, remained in existence throughout the Roman period, but seems to have declined in importance in the second century. The main Roman road through Verulamium was Watling Street, which ran directly from London (beyond that from the Channel ports of Dover and Richborough) and continued on to Chester.

Watling Street was presumably the route used by Suetonius Paulinus at the time of the Boudiccan revolt, although whether it was fully metalled at this period is uncertain (**32**). At Verulamium it does not seem to have been laid out in its metalled form until the

later Neronian or early Flavian period. Outside the built-up area of the town, Watling Street was a carefully engineered trunk road. Here it was 15m wide and flanked by widely spaced ditches, over 1m deep and set 9m away from the edge of the metalled surface. This layout provided unmetalled tracks suitable for unshod horses alongside a central metalled surface for wheeled vehicles; the flanking ditches ensured that the route was kept free of encroaching buildings, livestock and vegetation. That this arrangement was carefully maintained throughout the Roman period is demonstrated in the St Stephen's cemetery, 500m outside Roman Verulamium, where the widely spaced ditches flanking the road were repeatedly recut over two centuries, and all burials, pits and funerary structures kept firmly outside them. This wide road zone did not, however, occur inside the built-up area of the town. Here Watling Street was simply a well-metalled, carefully cambered urban street. When Watling Street was first laid out the built-up area of Verulamium was still comparatively small; this is why the street appears to cut diagonally across the line of the normal street grid in the southern part of the town. Furthermore, its widely spaced flanking ditches, characteristic of the street in its 'extramural' form, have been shown to underlie early second-century buildings in insulae I, II and under the triangular temple in insula VII. However, they do not seem to have continued across insula III, and excavation in the south corner of insula XIII has shown that Watling Street never crossed this insula. This absence suggests that when Watling Street was constructed

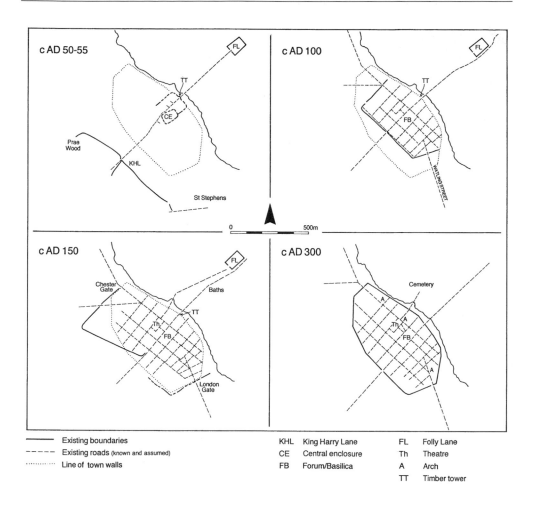

34 *The suggested development of Verulamium between the mid-first and later third centuries.*
Drawn by David Williams

the Roman town already extended, or was expected to extend, as far south as insula III (*see* **43** for the positions of the various insulae). That this expansion did not take place until after the Boudiccan revolt is demonstrated by the absence of mid-first-century occupation in insulae XVIII and XIII and by the presence of early Flavian pottery in the filling of the east arms of the Central Enclosure and annexe ditches. Both ditches on this side of the town were clearly still open throughout the 60s, and it was not until they were filled, at least in part, in the early Flavian period, that the built-up area extended south-east (**34**).

Once underway, however, expansion of the town was very rapid. At sometime in the later Neronian period, a substantial bank and ditch were constructed on three sides of the new town. This earthwork is generally referred to as the '1955 ditch' after the year in which it was first recognised. The ditch was 3-3.5m deep, 6m wide at its mouth with a steep, V-shaped profile (**33**). It ran around the south, east and west sides of the settlement, but was absent on the north; here the marshy valley floor must have been considered a sufficient boundary in itself, although in insulae XVII and XIX this would have been augmented by the earlier turf and timber bank which was still standing. The area enclosed in this way covered just over 100 acres (75ha). It has not proved easy to date the 1955 ditch precisely. When first excavated it was thought that it might initially have been dug in the pre-Boudiccan period, and that it represented the limits of the first, post-conquest town. The problem is caused by the absence of a bank. Presumably the material dug out of the ditch was piled up beside it to provide a rampart. Had this survived it could have been expected to contain contemporary material, and to seal earlier remains beneath it, thus providing a reasonable indication of its initial date. In this case, however, the bank had subsequently been used to level the ditch and so little of it remains that it is not even certain on which side of the ditch it stood. As a result the ditch's date can only be estimated on the basis of material found in its silt. Unfortunately, most of this material will only have accumulated once the ditch had ceased to be maintained and was being allowed to silt up, or while it was being finally filled in. It therefore provides a date, not for its construction, but for its abandonment. Even the 'primary' silt that accumulated soon after the ditch was first dug merely contained sherds that already had been lying on the surface for many years previously.

In fact the best evidence for the initial date of the 1955 ditch comes not from the ditch itself, but from the expanding settlement within its circuit. The southern part of the area enclosed includes insulae I-VIII, all areas crossed by Watling Street in its 'extramural' form with widely spaced flanking ditches. In other words, this length of Watling Street was laid out when Verulamium was still a small settlement focused around the Central Enclosure. By the time the 1955 ditch came to be dug it had become clear that the town was destined to be substantially larger, and a number of extra insulae had to be allowed for on its south-eastern side (**34**). Apart from the area around insula VII where there is a small concentration of conquest period pottery, coins and brooches suggesting a possible sacred area, the earliest buildings in these insulae are associated with pottery produced at Bricket Wood (3km south-east of Verulamium) and Highgate Wood (north of London). Although the Bricket Wood kiln was operating in the 50s, those at Highgate Wood were not producing the sandy grey wares found in the southern part of Verulamium until about AD 70. On present evidence therefore the most likely date for the construction of the 1955 ditch is *c.*AD 75-80. It therefore represents a very rapid expansion of the town in the later Neronian and early Flavian periods.

It is possible that the diagonal course of Watling Street in the southern part of later first-century Verulamium was mirrored on the west by a road leading to Wood Lane End, Cow Roast and Akeman Street. This road would have entered Verulamium from the south-west across a causeway in the New Dyke, a short distance east of Gorhambury. After the mid-second century this road branched off Watling Street immediately outside the Chester Gate, but in 2000 a small geophysical survey by English Heritage in insula XXXVI revealed what appear to be property boundaries on an oblique line to that of the main street grid. These could reflect an early line of the Wood Lane End/Cow Roast road, a line which brought the road across the White Dyke, through the otherwise unexplained gap in the Fosse ditch 340m south-west of the Chester Gate[21] to join Watling Street near the point at which it crossed the 1955 ditch (**34** & **43**).

Flavian Verulamium

Central to the area defined by the 1955 ditch was the Forum/Basilica complex, the commercial and administrative centre of the town. This stood on the site of the earlier Central Enclosure, and today its remains lie buried beneath St Michael's church and vicarage. Since 1955 the Forum/Basilica has been dated on the basis of a fragmentary inscription found in that year on the opposite side of Watling Street, during building work in St Michael's School. Unfortunately all the surviving fragments were retrieved after they had already been removed from the ground by the builders, so their true stratigraphical position is unknown. They had probably been lying in the layer of rubble derived from the demolition and robbing of the Basilica in the post-Roman period. Although less than 20% of the inscription survives, the full text has been restored and dated to the autumn of 79 during the governorship of Julius Agricola.[22] The details of the reconstruction are still a matter of debate; indeed it now appears that the fragments derive from two separate inscriptions. Nevertheless, it is clear that the inscription, or inscriptions, commemorated the completion of a major public building during the period of Agricola's governorship (AD 78-85).

The plan of the Forum/Basilica complex as we know it today is the result of less than half a dozen excavations, some very small-scale, that have been undertaken at various times between 1898 and 1998. A little additional information can be gleaned from records made during repairs to St Michael's Church in 1897-8 and notes made by F.T. Negus, the City Engineer in the early 1930s (**35**). Most of the remains lie 2-3m below the modern surface, and apart from the inscription, dating evidence remains extremely scanty. The most extensive areas of excavation were those in the Forum in the early years of the twentieth century by William Page, and the vicar of St Michael's, Charles Bicknell,[23] and those by A.W.G. Lowther and P.G. Corder in the 1930s on the east corner of the Basilica.[24]

As a result of this work the overall layout of the Forum/Basilica complex is clear, but there remains considerable uncertainty about the detail of its plan. The complex covered a double insula, giving it a total area of over 2,000m². It consisted of a large colonnaded courtyard with a temple opening off its south-west side and a small temple or, more probably, a *curia* (council chamber) at its south corner; a second temple was built, at the west corner in the late-second century.[25] The Basilica stood on the north-east side of the court, between it and Watling Street.

Most of our information comes from excavations carried out between 1902 and 1911 by Page and Bicknell. In 1914 Page published a plan of the complex showing the Forum with centrally placed entrances on the south-east and north-west. Unfortunately this plan contained a mistake. Measurements had apparently been taken from the Victorian vicarage. The Vicarage was shown on the published plan but placed some 12m too far to the south-west. The mistake was pointed out by Bicknell in a letter to Page in 1911, but for some reason it was never rectified. The situation became still more confused when the vicarage

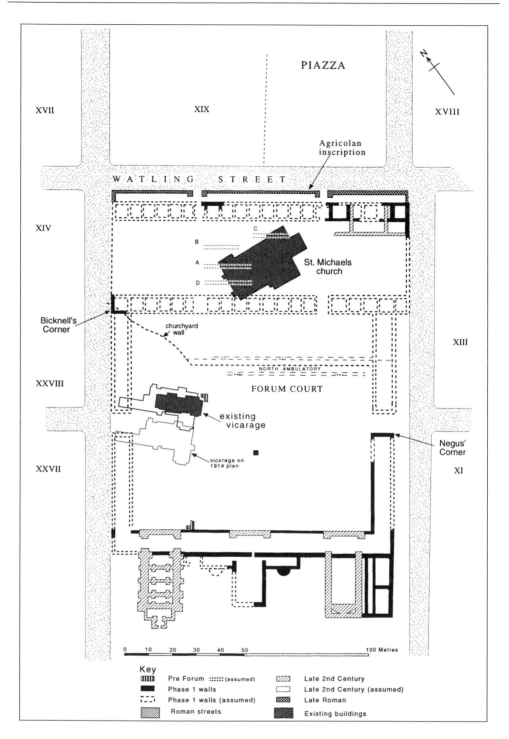

35 Plan of the Forum/Basilica complex, including information derived from Rev Bicknell and Mr Negus. The early twentieth-century mistake over the relative positions of the vicarage and the entrances into the Forum court has been rectified here. Drawn by Philip Dean

was rebuilt in the 1920s. Later archaeologists, attempting to check Page and Bicknell's findings, were forced to assume that the Vicarage had been rebuilt further north, whereas in fact comparison with the first edition Ordnance Survey map shows that the two buildings stood on virtually the same spot. As a result, from 1914 onwards, on all the plans of the Forum/Basilica the south-west side of the Forum court and the two entrances were also shown too far south-west. The situation is not clarified by the omission from any of Page and Bicknell's notes of a precise measurement of the distance of the south corner of the Forum court from the south-eastern entrance. Nevertheless, both Page and Bicknell were clearly agreed that the entrances were more or less opposite the Victorian vicarage. By placing the Victorian vicarage in its correct place on the plan, but at the same time retaining the central positions of the entrances into the court, we arrive at a Forum court approximately 88m long and 98m wide. A position for the south-east entrance approximately 12m further north-east of the position shown on the 1914 plan was confirmed by an observation made in 1930 by the city engineer, F.T. Negus. Negus' plan survives and shows a cross wall 31m south-west of the existing churchyard wall, more or less in the expected position for the south wall of the south-eastern entrance (**35**).

An increase of about 12m in the width of the Forum court means in turn that the width of the Basilica, on the north-east side of the court, has to be reduced by 12m. Fortunately there are records of two corners for the Basilica. The east corner was excavated in the 1930s by Lowther, and additional observations were recorded in 1939 by the first director of the Verulamium Museum, Philip Corder. The position of the west corner has only recently been recognised. It was recorded by Charles Bicknell in 1911 when a tree was dug out by his front gate, close to the churchyard wall. Admittedly the only surviving records consist of a sketch and a short description in a letter to Page, but these show that the corner was on the north side of the entrance drive into the Vicarage garden ('Bicknell's corner', **35**). Comparison with the Ordnance Survey map (first edition) which shows the position of the vicarage drive and front gate, allows the corner to be located with reasonable confidence and gives us a Basilica 45m wide and 120m long.

Any reconstruction of the Basilica has to accommodate the numerous walls that have been recorded running parallel to it longitudinally. Indeed, as one nineteenth-century historian complained, 'The whole churchyard seems to have a substratum of Roman masonry, and much difficulty has been experienced in digging graves by reason of the presence of these massive foundations . . .'.[26] Most of the walls on which we have any useful information were those recorded by Bicknell in 1897 during 'tidying up' work in the churchyard. He recorded three massive foundations, close to St Michael's church. The central wall of the three, running under the church tower, supported massive column drums in Barnack stone. Bicknell also recorded two further walls close to the existing churchyard wall. Yet two more lengths of longitudinal walls were excavated near the east corner of the Basilica in 1940 and 1955. The reconstructions of the Basilica that have been suggested in the past have all attempted to accommodate all these longitudinal walls into one structure. It is clear however that the whole Forum/Basilica complex was rebuilt, in most places from the ground up, in the later part of the second century, so there is no reason why all these walls should be contemporary. Indeed, in the case of the walls at the east corner of the Basilica, excavation has demonstrated that they were not all contemporary.[27] The evidence provided by Bicknell's west corner also makes it clear that at some stage the Basilica was only 45m wide, compared to the 60.9m required if the walls near the edge of the vicarage garden are included, as they invariably have been in all reconstructions since 1914. With such a wealth of walls, few of which have been precisely planned, numerous reconstructions are possible for the Basilica at Verulamium. Frustratingly, all of them are largely conjectural. However, a possible reconstruction of the complex, incorporating the corrections made to Page's 1914 plan, is shown on figure **35**. Here it is suggested in its first phase that the Forum/Basilica complex consisted of a courtyard, measuring 88m by 98m with two centrally placed entrances. At this phase the surrounding wall was built of dressed blocks of Barnack stone with an internal colonnade supported by columns built of segmental tiles, faced with white plaster. Similar tiles were used for the colonnade surrounding the late first-century precinct in the insula XVI temple (see below p78). The Basilica in phase 1 had a row of rooms along its north-eastern side, just over 6m wide and with two entrances opening onto Watling Street. On figure **35** it is assumed that Bicknell's west corner represents one end of a similar range on the south-west, and that two of the walls observed in the churchyard in 1897 (Wall A, the dwarf walls with Barnack stone columns under the church tower, and wall B, about 4m to the north) supported a central nave. Excavations in 1939 and 1972 near the east corner of the Basilica showed that in phase 2 this earlier range of small rooms was replaced by three larger rooms, over 10m wide. It is also assumed that both ranges were rebuilt in this way, and that walls C and D, recorded by Bicknell beneath the church and outside its west door, belong to the enlarged rooms of phase 2. Whether the central, colonnaded nave was rebuilt at this phase is unknown. Other changes in phase 2 were the addition of temples on the south-west side of the Forum court.

There remains the problem posed by the walls recorded by Bicknell close to the edge of the vicarage garden, his 'north ambulatory' in the Forum courtyard. It is not known how much of these walls were actually exposed; the surviving plans show only short lengths towards the centre of the court. It is possible that these are part of the still earlier building that is known to underlie the south-west part of the court. These early walls have already been referred (p65) when it was suggested that they could have belonged to an early or proto-Forum, substantially smaller than the phase 1 complex.

The question also arises as to which phase of building the fragmentary inscription belongs. Clearly the phase 2 Forum/Basilica is out of the question, dating as it does to the later second century. The inscription could however derive from the early 'proto-Forum', which in this case would have been constructed in the post- rather than pre-Boudiccan period. This would make it contemporary with the wooden proto-Forum at London. The proto-Forum at London was replaced by a much larger Forum/Basilica in the early second century, between about 100 and 130. A similar sequence at Verulamium would mean the proto-Forum being dismantled in the Hadrianic period, after a life of 30 or 40 years, and the Agricolan inscription being broken up and incorporated in the new, extended building. This building would have then been destroyed within a few years of completion in the fire of 155.

It has to be admitted however, that without further excavation, of which, in view of the site of the complex, and the depth at which the remains lie, there is not the remotest prospect, our knowledge of the details of the Forum/Basilica is unlikely to increase. If nothing else, figure **35** serves as an illustration of how little is really known of the Verulamium Forum/Basilica in spite of it being dated by inscription, and after a century of recorded observations.

Other public buildings and works

Whatever its plan, the late first-century Forum/Basilica, with its Agricolan inscription beautifully cut on large slabs of Purbeck marble, must have formed an impressive and prestigious centre-piece to the town. Around it the old annexe and Central Enclosure ditches were levelled and the nucleus of the rectilinear street grid that was to serve the town for the next three centuries was laid out. The streets were now carefully cambered and metalled and in many cases bordered on both sides by planked gullies; these probably carried off waste from private houses as well as surface water from the streets. By the last quarter of the first century a flint and mortar conduit brought water from the river Ver to the north of insula XVII; this may have supplied fountains along Watling Street, as parts of two large Purbeck marble basins have been recorded in insulae XVII and VIII. Timber water pipes from insulae II, XVIII and XXVIII suggest that the lower lying insulae of the town had a piped water supply by the end of the first century. Although a few wells have been reported from the town, they never seem to have been numerous; some of the so-called wells may really have been shafts dug for religious or votive reasons.

Many of the public buildings in the town date from the late first century. In 1988 a small trench was excavated in the north corner of insula III. It was dug primarily in order to establish whether or not Watling Street had ever crossed the insula diagonally, but it also encountered what was almost certainly part of the public Baths. The excavated remains consisted of parts of three rooms associated with two massive, vaulted drains; one room included a hypocaust. The rubble, resulting from the destruction of the building, contained numerous small toilet objects — dress pins and tweezers as well as a short ceramic tube of the type used to conduct hot air around the vaulted roof of bath buildings. These finds, combined with the scale of the drain and the massive nature of the associated wall foundations, all suggested that this was part of a public rather than private bathhouse. Dating evidence was not plentiful, but the small quantity of pottery found sealed beneath the building showed that it could not have been built earlier than the late Flavian period. The earlier bathhouse in insula XIX seems to have continued in use until the end of the first century, making it reasonable to suggest that the insula III building replaced it, probably sometime in the reign of Trajan (98-117).

North-west of the Forum a large *macellum* or market hall was built in insula XVII. It covered an area of 400m² and dated from *c*.AD 85. The *macellum* consisted two ranges of box-like compartments on opposite sides of a central courtyard, across which ran the conduit bringing water from the river, 180m to the north. *Macella* were generally associated with meat markets; at Verulamium substantial concentrations of animal bones have been recorded during field walking and in service trenches north and east of the *macellum*. Certainly the *macellum* at this phase appears to have been a rather utilitarian building (but *see* **58** for a later version).

Numerous temples are known or suspected from Verulamium and its outskirts. In addition to the two temples on the south side of the Forum courtyard, five temples are known from within the area of the Roman town. With a central, square or rectangular *cella*, surrounded by a portico or veranda, these are all of the 'Romano-Celtic' type, typical of both Roman Britain and Gaul. In Verulamium, the plan of the so-called triangular temple in insula VII was adapted in order to fit the unusually shaped insula, caused by the diagonal course of Watling Street in this area. Only two of the Romano-Celtic temples have seen any excavation, and only in the case of the triangular temple was this excavation extensive. Both the triangular temple and the large temple in insula XVI were first built in the last quarter of the first century, although both stand on sites where there is a concentration of earlier material, such as pre-Roman coins and early brooches. Coins and brooches were commonly left as offerings on ritual sites, and their presence here may be an indication that both sites were regarded as sacred places long before the temples themselves were built. Other Romano-Celtic temples in insulae XVII and XXI are known only from air photographs so their date remains unknown (**36**).

The area immediately north-east of the insula XVI temple was maintained as an open, gravelled area throughout the late first and early second century. It was probably used for public gatherings and events associated with the temple. In about 140 however, this open court was replaced by a timber theatre. The Verulamium theatre is a typical example of the provincial, Romano-Gallic type of Roman theatre. Instead of a semicircular auditorium, or *cavea*, facing a large stage and with a small central area (the *orchestra*), the Verulamium stage was small and the wings of the *cavea* so extended that nearly a fifth of the seats must have faced the enlarged, arena-like *orchestra* rather than the stage. Like classical theatres these provincial theatres were associated with temples, and were used as much for religious or ritual events, or games, as for dramatic performances.

Private houses and workshops

Most private houses in the town remained relatively modest throughout the later first and early second centuries. Unfortunately only a few complete buildings have been exposed, and no occupation site within the town has been excavated in its entirety, that is with all its associated outbuildings, yards and storage areas. Such buildings as have been exposed fully are those in insula XIV and XXVIII on the north-west side of the Forum. The workshops on the Watling Street frontage in insula XIV (all of which had been completely destroyed in the Boudiccan revolt) were not rebuilt for some 15 years; in the interval the site was unoccupied. Nevertheless, when finally rebuilt, the late first-century buildings followed lines very similar to those of their predecessors, and were used by metalworkers for very similar purposes. Early second-century lathe emplacements in two workshops occupied the same relative positions as had their predecessors.[28] Elsewhere, buildings in insulae XVIII and XIII suggest that rectangular houses, with two or three rooms, were the norm. Traditional building methods continued. Buildings were timber-framed and supported on sleeper beams laid directly on the ground surface, or set into shallow slots. Between the timber uprights the walls were either made of wattle hurdles, smeared with clay and then usually plastered, or clay tamped down between two planks or hurdles. Floors were of beaten earth or chalk or were planked, and increasingly roofs were tiled.

36 Aerial view taken in July 1976 of the Verulamium theatre. The photograph shows the later Roman stage encroaching into the large, mid-second-century orchestra. In the foreground the plan of a Romano-Celtic temple in insula XVII shows clearly as crop-marks. Copyright St Albans Museum

The late first-century expansion of the town (discussed above) presumably reflects a substantially larger population. Who were these people and where did they come from? Without undertaking numerous large-scale excavations it is impossible to measure the relative density of occupation in the town and its hinterland. Much of the information on rural sites that we have is based on little more than collections of pottery made during field-walking surveys or as chance finds. In cases where substantial quantities of first-century pottery are recorded the material tends to date until about AD 85-100, after which the series abruptly cease. While this may mean that occupation on the site ceased, and the former inhabitants moved somewhere completely different, it is also possible that the

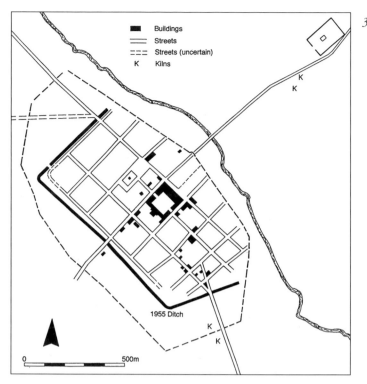

37 *Occupation in early second-century Verulamium.* Drawn by David Williams

first-century buildings were only relocated very slightly, and were rebuilt on adjacent sites, with the area under cultivation remaining much the same and with the same families farming it. On a number of local sites, such as Gorhambury, Mackerye End, Park Street and probably Childwickbury, occupation continued unbroken from the pre-Roman period, and villas ultimately developed here. At the same time on at least three sites, Gadebridge, Boxmoor and Kings Langley, late first-century farms were established on previously unoccupied land. Overall the number of sites where occupation may have ceased at the end of the first century may have been more or less cancelled out by the number of sites where occupation continued or was established for the first time.

It is clear from a glance at any plan of late first- or early second-century Verulamium that there were numerous apparently unoccupied areas separating the widely scattered buildings (**37-8**). The plans, however, are probably deceptive. The remains of buildings at this date for the most part lie a metre or more below the modern surface, and are often obscured by later structures, if not actually destroyed by them. The early buildings of the town have not been excavated to the same extent as the more visually impressive remains of the second and third centuries, and as they were generally built of timber they do not show up on aerial photographs. It is unfortunate that so little is known about the plots in which the buildings stood. This is true of all periods of Roman Verulamium, but is especially regrettable in the early years of the town. We have seen how in the pre-Roman period even a 'high-status' site like Gorhambury was surrounded by a host of auxiliary buildings and set in spacious ditched enclosures. The overall pattern of other enclosures in the area suggests that this may have been the normal pattern of local occupation, and

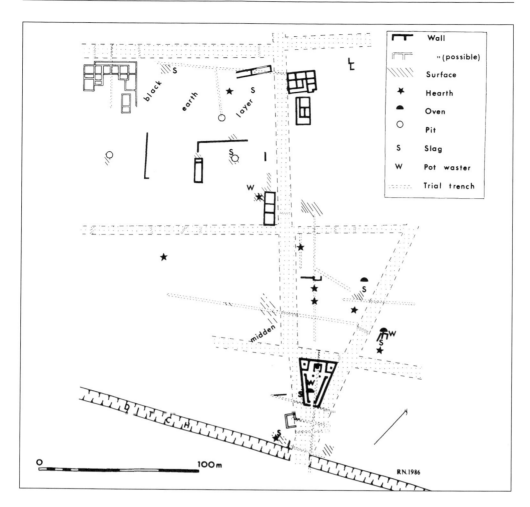

38 Early second-century occupation in insulae I-V. Drawing R. Niblett

similar arrangements are hinted at by the double enclosures at Pond Field, Mayne Avenue and Beaumont Hall Farm. Whether enclosures with accommodation for livestock, storage and workshops surrounded the late first-century buildings within the town itself is impossible to say. At least some buildings, however, appear to have been associated with open air working areas, and the short lengths of boundary ditches that have occasionally been recorded in the town may well be the remains of animal pens, paddocks or gardens.

Verulamium was not alone in its rapid expansion in the later first century; most towns in southern England saw a tremendous surge in building activity in these years. At Verulamium this rapid expansion continued into the first half of the second century. The 1955 ditch stopped being maintained in the early years of the second century when sections of it were filled in to allow houses to extend over it; by *c.*150-70 it was being systematically levelled. It was replaced by an earthwork defining an area at least twice as large and known as the Fosse.

The Fosse

Opinions vary as to the date and extent of the Fosse, and the problems associated with it are by no means resolved. The earthwork consisted of a ditch, 13m wide and 4m deep with a substantial bank on the inner side, and a smaller counter-scarp bank on the outer. Today it survives in private land just outside the west sector of the town, where it forms a triangular projection beyond the line of the later town wall. It has been badly eroded by ploughing but rather more survived in the Wheelers' day, and they were able to excavate trenches across its southern arm, at its western corner, and near the point at which it met Watling Street.[29] Although the section close to Watling Street had been disturbed by a later Roman chalk pit, in the other trenches the base of the banks still survived, and the Wheelers were able to excavate complete sections across both banks and ditch (**39**). On the south-west side of insula XXV they demonstrated that the Fosse pre-dated the third-century town wall. The 1930s excavations also located what appeared to be the southern corner of the Fosse between insulae XX and XXV. This led to the suggestion that originally the earthwork had run from the south corner of insula XXV, north-east towards the river, eventually joining the line of the later town wall somewhere in insula XIX. The road down Bluehouse Hill, which in the 1930s was a sunken lane, would have masked the earthwork over much of this course, and even though trial trenches cut in insula XIX failed to locate it,[30] this hypothetical line was taken by the Wheelers as marking the south-eastern boundary of the early second-century town (**8**).

This view of the Fosse was generally accepted until the discovery of the 1955 ditch and the Agricolan inscription from the Forum/Basilica showed that the town had already expanded south and east in the later first century and made the whole idea of a boundary along the line of Bluehouse Hill totally untenable. Excavations by Sheppard Frere in insula XX in the 1950s failed to find any continuation of the Fosse east of the corner in insula XXV, and Frere suggested that although the earthwork had been intended to run east to insula IX and the London Gate, it had never been completed. However, this theory does not explain the corner found by the Wheelers in insula XXV; nor does it explain the clear evidence found by the Wheelers that the inner bank of the Fosse had been substantially strengthened on at least one occasion. In its original form the gravel bank was 7m wide and was revetted at the rear with turf. The bank had then become grassed over, and a turf line developed. Subsequently the earthwork was widened, and presumably heightened, by the addition of further deposits of clay and gravel giving it at total width of 13m.[31] It is very difficult to reconcile this evidence for the strengthening of the bank with the argument that the Fosse was never completed. It has also been suggested that the Fosse was originally a pre-conquest earthwork that was refurbished in the second century.[32] This interpretation however, attractive as it is, fails because the pottery that the Wheelers found beneath the core of the original bank included several sherds that cannot have been produced before the last quarter of the first century AD.

The answer to the problem may be that the Fosse was in fact completed, and that it enclosed an even larger area than that suggested by Frere, and larger than the 201 acres (81.2ha) enclosed by the third-century town walls. Since Frere concluded his excavations, two lengths of ditch, both apparently dating to the second century, have been excavated on

39 The Fosse ditch during excavation by the Wheelers in 1932. Copyright St Albans Museum

the south-east side of the town. Both ditches lay close to the third-century town ditch, but both clearly pre-dated it. The first indication of a second-century ditch on this side of the town was found during the excavation of the Verulam Hills Field site in 1963/4. Here a substantial ditch, ditch IV, was excavated by B.F. Rawlins, but its description was for some reason omitted from the published report on the excavation.[33] The ditch was approximately 10m wide and nearly 3m deep; the excavation showed it had first been dug in about the middle of the second century, and after about a metre of silt had accumulated in its base, it had been deliberately filled. Another length of what may well have been the same ditch was found in 1980 by Chris Saunders on the south side of the town, a short distance north-east of its south corner. Trenches here revealed the eastern lip of a substantial ditch, running north-east, with traces of a 10m wide bank on its outer edge. The bank sealed a small quantity of material dating from the late first to early second centuries. This outer bank could well correspond to the counter-scarp bank of the Fosse. This may also be the explanation for the substantial ditch that still survives south-west of the main town ditch near the south corner of the town and which is shown on the Wheelers' published sections as a 'median' ditch (**34 & 37**).[34]

If we are correct in assuming that the Fosse originally enclosed the whole south-eastern half of Verulamium, the Wheelers' corner in the earthwork in insula XXV can be seen as one side of an in-turned entrance on the line of the street on the north-west side of the Forum. Until the middle of the second century this street continued to be the main road through the town linking the river crossing outside the 'Timber Tower' with the causeway through the Wheeler ditch in Pond Field.

The only reliable dating evidence for the Fosse is provided by the pottery contained in, or sealed under, the bank. Most of the pottery in the Verulamium Museum labelled as coming from the Fosse in fact was found in silt in the ditch. The bulk of this dates from the mid-first century AD, and is doubtless rubbish derived from the Prae Wood site. The same is true for much of the material from within or beneath the bank. A handful of sherds however was found lying on the old ground surface beneath the core of the bank. These sherds date from no earlier than the very end of the first century, so demonstrating conclusively the early second century as the earliest possible date for the construction of the Fosse. The most reasonable view is that the Fosse dates from the second quarter of the second century, at a time when the 1955 ditch was being extensively back filled and built over.

The entrances which brought Watling Street through the Fosse and into the town from the south-east and north-west were marked by the London and Chester Gates respectively. Both gates were excavated by the Wheelers, who dated them to the reign of Hadrian (117-138), a date which, with minor adjustments, is still generally accepted today. They clearly pre-dated the third-century town walls, which abutted them on either side, and are almost certainly contemporary with the Fosse earthwork. These gates were imposing structures. They consisted of double carriageways, each 3.5m wide flanked by narrower footways and surmounted by massive gate houses, supported by projecting drum towers. They would have provided prestigious entrances into what was now an expanding and prosperous town (**40**).

The Fosse earthwork, quite possibly enclosing an area of over 200ha and completed in *c*.140, provides a vivid illustration of the way in which Verulamium continued to expand throughout the first half of the second century. Together with the other public works, it is evidence of the way in which the Catuvellaunian notables of the late first and second centuries proclaimed the importance of their tribal capital, while at the same time boosting their own personal prestige by financing ostentatious public works, embellished no doubt by appropriate inscriptions advertising their generosity. Although all that survives today are their heavily robbed flint and mortar foundations, in their day both the London and the Chester gates were imposing structures, expressly designed to impress anyone approaching the town along Watling Street. Indeed visitors to the town in about 150 could scarcely fail to be impressed. Entering the town through the London Gate they would have been confronted by an enormous projecting gatehouse, towering over the road. The flint and mortar walls were probably originally faced with sandstone and would almost certainly have carried a monumental inscription. Once into the town, visitors would soon have reached one of the two points at which Watling Street crossed

40 The Chester Gate during excavation (1931) when the foundations for the large projecting drum tower on the south-west side of Watling Street was exposed. Photograph St Albans Museum Service

the 1955 ditch, now in the process of being levelled. In the third century these points were each marked by a monumental arch marking the boundaries of the earlier *municipium*. Presumably, since these points were still known a century after the ditch had been filled in, they had been marked in some way throughout the second century. Next, visitors would have been confronted by the triangular temple in insula VII. Dedicated to Cybele, whose role, among others, was the protection of towns, this temple had an external altar facing the fork where the diagonal line of Watling Street joined the main street grid. The plastered walls of the temple, in this case probably embellished with Purbeck marble, fragments of which were found in the 1930s' excavations, provided a backdrop to the altar. Beyond the temple were the massive walls of the public baths whose domed roof must have risen well above the tiled roofs of the surrounding houses, still largely built of lath and plaster. North-west of the Baths stood the Forum/Basilica complex. If, as is possible, this had been rebuilt on an extended plan in the Hadrianic period, it would have been almost contemporary with the Fosse and the two Gatehouses, representing massive investment in public works in the second quarter of the second century. Leaving the Forum court by its north-west gate, visitors would have found themselves in streets whose frontages were closely built up with timber framed shops and workshops. Many of these were typical of the type of buildings now spreading over much

85

41 Bronze bowl from a late first-century burial on the northern edge of the King Harry Lane cemetery. Maximum diameter 16.2cm. Photograph St Albans Museum Service

of the ground once enclosed by the 1955 ditch. As in the Forum area, most of them stood on street frontages, with their narrower ends opening onto the streets; inside, the front rooms were generally used as shops while the backrooms served as workshops, stores and living quarters. Behind the buildings themselves, and sometimes reached by narrow lanes, were open areas or yards, containing pits for cess or rubbish, hearths and ovens. Some may have been partially roofed and it is not difficult to imagine these being used as general purpose utility areas, serving as places to keep extra materials, firewood and carts, for open air cooking and industrial activities, and for accommodating livestock, such as the hens, pigs, mules and donkeys with which the town must have abounded. Pressing on along Watling Street, visitors would have passed between the newly-constructed timber theatre on their left (now masking the large temple behind it) and on their right, the entrance into the *macellum,* a timber building now more than 50 years old, and perhaps beginning to show signs of wear. Visitors finally left Verulamium through the Chester Gate, 550m further along Watling Street, and an almost identical twin of the London Gate over a kilometre to the south-east.

Mid-second-century Verulamium was a thriving and expanding town. The public building programme itself is evidence of the wealth of the Catuvellaunian landowners and the local merchants. The enthusiastic way in which the British aristocracy had adopted Roman lifestyles in the later first century was commented on by Tacitus and this attitude clearly persisted in the second century. It has been argued that this, combined with a desire to out-do rivals in demonstrating their wealth by financing prestigious public works and entertainments, replaced the traditional ways in which the tribal aristocracy had competed — by fighting and throwing lavish feasts. The feasting, in the form of extravagant dinner parties, however, no doubt continued. One of the most evocative finds of recent years was

42 *Bronze model of a dinner party guest found in the river silt close to the trackway from the 'Timber Tower'. A possible alternative identification is as a river or water deity. Maximum width 3.1cm.* Photograph St Albans Museum Service

the chance discovery in 1989 of a wealthy burial (**colour plate 9**). Its position under a centuries-old field bank had protected it from destruction by ploughing and erosion. The burial dated from about AD 85. It was that of an elderly individual who must have lived through both the Roman conquest and the Boudiccan revolt. He may well have witnessed the funeral of the chieftain buried on the Folly Lane site, the transformation of the Central Enclosure into the earliest Forum/Basilica complex, the construction of the insula XIX baths and the surge of building that took place once the area had recovered from the events of 61. He was evidently a person of wealth and standing, but he was buried with none of the traditional ceremony evident at Folly Lane. Instead he went to the grave with a complete samian dinner service imported from South Gaul, an ornate bronze bowl made in Gaul or Italy and probably used for mixing wine, an iron-framed folding chair, glass flasks and jars, two iron strigils, four lamps and a set of gaming counters. The whole group of objects characterises the equipment needed for a formal dinner party from the bathing beforehand to the elaborate rituals of serving wine (**41**). The chair, a Roman symbol of magisterial rank, completes the picture of a successful native dignitary quick to adopt the now fashionable Roman lifestyle. A similar but rather less sophisticated picture is provided by a tiny bronze model of a dinner party guest, found in a marshy deposit close to the 'Timber Tower' (**42**).

Alongside the massive public building programme was a gradual rise in the level of sophistication and comfort in many of the private houses. By the beginning of the second century flint and mortar foundations were already being used in some houses, and many had solid mortar or *opus signinum* floors. Roofs were now almost invariably tiled, and walls plastered and painted with plain, coloured washes sometimes enlivened by bands of red, green or yellow. Increasingly extra rooms were added to strip buildings, often connected with corridors or verandas. Nevertheless it has been suggested that the standard of domestic building in early second-century Verulamium lagged behind that in the surrounding countryside. This of course only applies to the houses of the wealthy. The houses of the rural poor in Roman Britain generally, and in the Verulamium area in particular, have not attracted the attention of excavators until very recently; consequently we know very little about them. There is however no reason to suppose that they were more Romanised or of a higher standard than those of the bulk of the population of Verulamium. Many of the second-century strip buildings in Verulamium may appear very simple when described in an excavation report, but no doubt a modern estate agent, miraculously transported back to the reign of Hadrian, would describe them as 'offering spacious and well-planned family accommodation with potential for further improvement'.

4 The town and its people
The second and third centuries

The death of the emperor Hadrian in 138 and the succession of Antoninus Pius saw the start of the Antonine period. Under Antoninus, and his successor Marcus Aurelius, the Empire was at the height of its power; it covered an area reaching from central Scotland to the Sahara and from Wales to Palestine and Romania. Most areas within its boundaries experienced a prolonged period of peace and stability. It was only on the murder of Marcus Aurelius' unstable son Commodus in 192 that the Antonine period ended in disruption and civil war.

By the end of Hadrian's reign Verulamium had all the attributes of a major provincial town within the Empire. Spatially the town had reached what was to be its greatest extent. On Watling Street the London and Chester Gates provided imposing entrances into a busy settlement, dominated by the enormous Forum/Basilica complex (**colour plates 10-11**). The baths and *macellum* were complete and functioning. Although the Fosse earthwork was either complete or nearing completion, the need to defend the town from hostile attack must have seemed a remote eventuality. Consequently we must assume that the Fosse 'defence' was constructed more with an eye to emphasising the importance of the Catuvellaunian capital than for its protection. Shortly after the construction of the Fosse, however, the town suffered a major disaster. Between about 155 and 160 an intense fire swept through the lower part of the town, destroying everything in a great swathe reaching from insulae II and V in the south to insulae XXXVI-VII in the north. There is no reason to think that the fire was not started accidentally but at least a third of the built-up area was affected. Excavations have recovered traces of over 30 buildings destroyed at this time, although this must be only a fraction of the total number. Most of these were timber-framed but not even masonry-built public buildings were immune. The Forum, Basilica, Baths and the 'triangular' temple in insula VII were all destroyed. As the buildings had been hastily abandoned, leaving behind tools, stores and furniture, the thick layer of burnt debris that covers many of the remains provides the archaeologist with a snapshot of the town in the mid-second century (**44, colour plate 12**).

By the mid-second century much of the area within the (by now largely invisible) 1955 ditch had been built up, at least along the street frontages. Along Watling Street in particular, buildings were closely packed. Unfortunately it is difficult to recover complete plans of these buildings; their clay and timber construction means they are not detectable from the air, and most have been overlain by later deposits. Only in 14 cases are reasonably complete plans of domestic buildings of this period available. While strip buildings were still being built and occupied (as they were to continue to be throughout the Roman

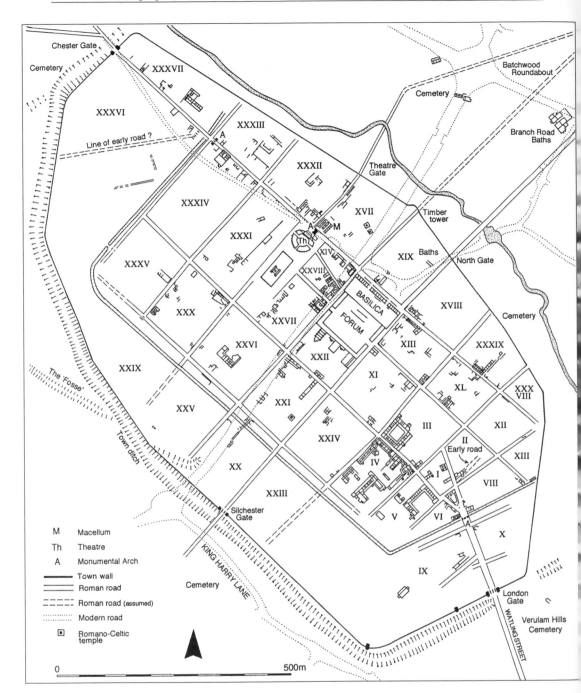

Chester Gate

Cemetery

XXXVII

XXXVI

Line of early road ?

XXXIII

XXXII

Theatre Gate

Cemetery

Batchwood Roundabout

Branch Road Baths

XXXIV

XXXI

XVII

Timber tower

XXXV

XXVIII

XIV

Th

M

A

XIX

Baths

North Gate

XXX

XXVII

BASILICA

FORUM

XVIII

Cemetery

XXVI

XXII

XIII

XXXIX

XXIX

XI

XL

XXXVIII

XXV

XXI

III

XII

XIII

XXIV

II
Early road

VIII

XX

IV

I

XXIII

V

VI

X

Silchester Gate

The 'Fosse'

Town ditch

KING HARRY LANE

Cemetery

IX

London Gate

WATLING STREET

Verulam Hills Cemetery

M   Macellum
Th   Theatre
A   Monumental Arch
──── Town wall
════ Roman road
╌╌╌╌ Roman road (assumed)
·········· Modern road
▣   Romano-Celtic temple

0   500m

43 Plan of Verulamium. Drawn by David Williams

44 Burnt floor joists with remains of burnt floorboards (bottom left) from a workshop in insula XIV destroyed in the early Antonine fire of c.155. From a building in the south corner of insula XIII.
Reproduced courtesy of the St Albans Museum Service, copyright reserved

period), by the early Antonine period the domestic buildings in Verulamium show considerable variety in plan. The most fully excavated are those uncovered by Sheppard Frere on the north-east side of insula XIV, between the Forum/Basilica and the theatre.[1] Particularly interesting are the houses opening onto Watling Street through a shared portico. These stood on the site of the mid-first-century workshops destroyed in the Boudiccan revolt, and while several were still being used by metalworkers, in appearance they were very different (**45**). Rather than a continuous range, the workshops now comprised separate houses, some of them separated by narrow alleys containing planked wooden drains carrying water from the tiled roofs. These early Antonine buildings were considerably larger than the earlier workshops. While the rooms closest to Watling Street were of similar proportions, and indeed in the majority of cases the walls were built on virtually the same lines, additional rooms to the rear almost doubled the size of the buildings. In at least three cases these rear rooms were grouped around a small open yard. On the basis of crucibles found in a room opening onto the yard behind one house, Frere suggested it had been used as a store by a jeweler working and trading in the front rooms. It is tempting to see other rear rooms as the private living accommodation away from the street frontage. The yards themselves seem to have been purely functional, taken up by ovens and rubbish pits. An intriguing feature of these houses is the way in which the larger houses tended to alternate with smaller ones. What was the relationship between the occupants of the different houses? Were the smaller houses occupied by 'junior partners' of 'senior partners' living in the larger house, both with access to the yard and stores, or is

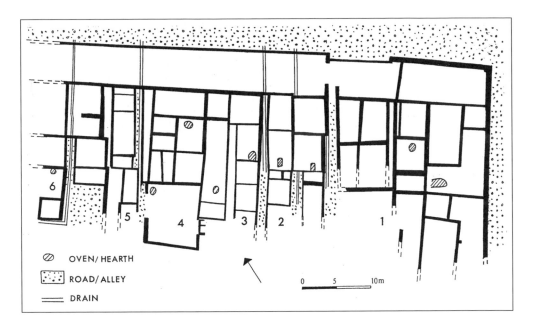

45 The workshops in insula XIV at the time of the Antonine Fire. Drawn by R. Niblett after Frere

this an example of joint ownership of property by two related families? Joint ownership, or at any rate joint occupancy, may explain the plan of one building in the range (building 2, **45**). Here a single building comprised two sets of almost identical rooms but with no internal access between them. To the rear two separate but similar wings opened onto a small, shared yard. This plan may reflect two separate but related families occupying a divided house.

The yards would have provided convenient open-air working areas adjacent to stores, but the width of the lanes that led to them from the rear would not have been sufficient to allow carts into them, and stores kept here must have been brought in by hand. This was not the case in a building, excavated in 1986-8, at the south corner of insula XIII.[2] From a commercial point of view this must have been a prime site. It lay on a street corner, diagonally opposite the town baths and on the direct route from the London Gate to the south-east entrance to the Forum. To the rear of the premises a wide entrance opening onto the street between insulae XIII and XL gave access to a yard largely taken up by a substantial oven and a flint-lined well. Seven rooms of various sizes opened onto the yard, some of them through porches or a covered portico. Some rooms contained traces of metalworking, including a small smithing furnace, but two were granaries with raised floors supported on large timber joists. On the south-west side of the building, three rooms opened onto the road leading to the Forum. In two of these were further traces of 'industrial activity' — two small ovens, a hearth and the base of some kind of wooden equipment supported by massive beams. Whether this was a press of some sort, or the remains of lifting gear, is unknown, but the base of a five-staved tub or barrel had been set

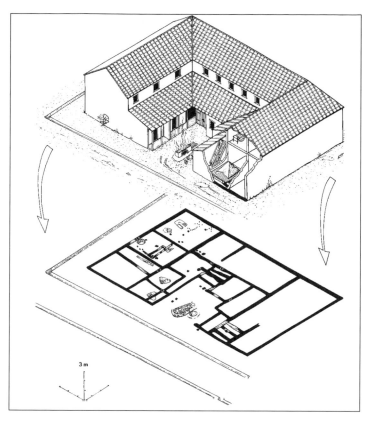

46 A mid-second-century building in the south corner of insula XIII as it may have looked shortly before the fire of c.155. Drawn by Alex Thorne

into the floor close by suggesting that whatever the process was, it required a supply of water close at hand. An adjacent stairwell indicated the presence of an upper storey (**colour plate 12**). The large hearth that took up so much of the space in the yard rested on an extremely solid chalk base, sunk half a metre into the subsoil. It was evidently designed to carry a considerable weight, and used for a process that required a constant supply of water; at a later stage it was provided with a small drain channeling surplus water into the drain along the side street. It is not difficult to image quantities of beer being brewed in this yard using water from the adjacent well and grain stored in the two granaries and gently warmed in the ovens in the south-west corner of the building. At the same time the rooms at the south end of the house were being used for metalworking, including the production or use of hundreds of tiny bronze rivets. Whether the kiln bar found in burnt debris over the north end of the building derives from one or other of the excavated hearths, or whether it is an indication of pottery kilns in the area is yet another question (**46**). The plan of this building resembles in some ways those of winged corridor villas (discussed below). There is no indication of a continuous connecting corridor, however, and the rooms opening onto the yard seem to have been added piecemeal to a house that had started life in the late first century as a simple strip building.

It is unfortunate that as in most other Romano-British towns, past excavations have concentrated on domestic houses and largely ignored the working areas and outbuildings that almost certainly surrounded them. We can reasonably assume that most houses in

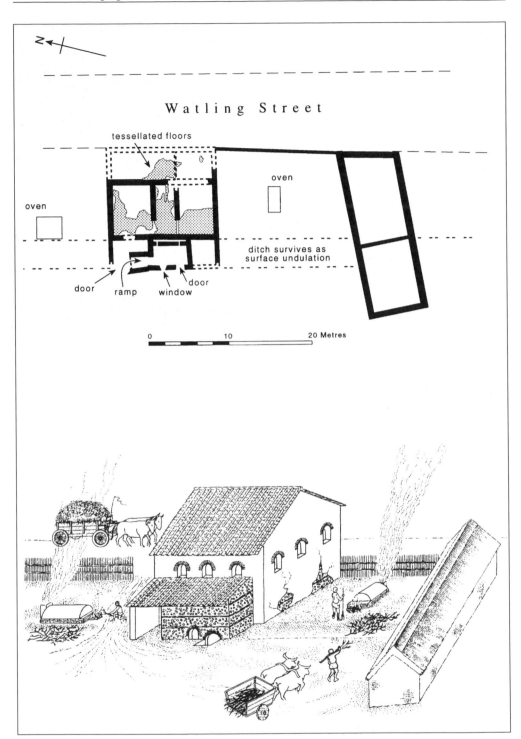

47 Building 1, insula I as it may have looked shortly after the fire of c.155. Drawn by Philip Dean

48 Building 1, insula I during excavation by the Wheelers in 1930. A blocked window and doorway into the basement room can be seen on the right; in the foreground is a ramp leading down into the same room. The holes in the walls of the room probably once supported shelves. Photograph St Albans Museum Service

Verulamium had such subsidiary buildings, many of them no doubt opening onto working areas and yards. A small building in insula I, excavated by the Wheelers in 1930 and dating to the late second or early third century, was probably typical of many houses in Verulamium.[3] The main residential house fronted onto Watling Street. It had flint and mortar footings and consisted of five rooms, most of them with plain red, tessellated floors. A wide entrance at the rear gave access to a sloping ramp leading down to a semi-basement room and presumably used as a store (**47**). East of the house a wall along Watling Street connected the main block with a two-roomed strip building and formed a partially enclosed yard. Very few details survive of the strip building, but it does not appear to have contained any hearths or ovens and may well have been another storehouse, or possibly a byre or stable. Associated with the house at this stage were two further examples of the type of large hearth on substantial foundations excavated in insula XIII (**48**).

Shops and workshops along the street frontages, with attached yards and storerooms to the rear, must have been common in second- and third-century Verulamium, but they were by no means the only type of domestic building. By the mid-second century a growing number of houses were planned as corridor buildings, with ranges of up to eight rooms opening off a connecting corridor. Sometimes these represent a modification of an earlier strip building. In insula XXVIII a corridor building, probably only just completed at the time of the fire, consisted of two ranges of rooms, both served by an L-shaped corridor.[4] The six rooms in the north range had mortar or tessellated floors, and one contained a mosaic and hypocaust (**colour plates 10-11**). In this range the walls were plastered and elaborately painted. By contrast the two rooms in the south range, fronting on the street, were less well appointed and probably served as a shop. This building, resting on flint and mortar footings and with its expensive internal decoration, is one of the most sophisticated domestic buildings known from the early Antonine town. It displays a clear differentiation between the private, residential quarters, and the working premises; indeed the two wings were separated by a doorway set at the angle of the corridor. The lack of objects from within the building suggests that the prospective occupants had not yet moved in when it was destroyed in the fire. They had clearly decided, however, that they were not going to be content with the sort of 'work-a-day' jumble of rooms grouped round the working yards that their neighbours occupied. Instead they insisted on a private wing of elegant rooms carefully separated from the business premises.

Inevitably there are a number of buildings from Verulamium that cannot be classified as strip buildings, 'yard' buildings or corridor buildings. These show considerable variation in size and plan but not infrequently they consist of simple square or rectangular blocks of several rooms, sometimes incorporating short corridors. Shortly before the outbreak of the early Antonine fire two small buildings of this type were built in the west corner of insula III, close to the public baths.[5] Like the corridor building in insula XXVIII, the construction of both houses was somewhat in advance of the general run of buildings in the town. Both rested on flint and mortar foundations and had solid mortar floors; the larger of the two had a small projecting porch leading into the largest of its eight rooms which was decorated with painted wall plaster (**49**).

In spite of the variety of buildings known from mid-second-century Verulamium, two types of houses are conspicuously absent at this period. The first are roundhouses. Although common in the area in the pre-conquest period, none are known from the Roman town. This is in spite of the fact that it is becoming increasingly clear that this type of house continued to be built and occupied in southern Britain, at least until the third century. Although predominantly rural in their distribution, at London, less than a day's ride along Watling Street, roundhouses were still being built in the Antonine period. In Verulamium however there is no sign of them; even where all that survives of houses are the clay or gravel floors, these invariably have straight, not curved, edges. Third-century roundhouses on the nearby villa site at Gorhambury were interpreted as either storerooms or the houses of lower status farm workers. If living in a roundhouse was really a sign of inferior status it may tell us something of the comparative wealth of the town population.

Also notably absent are the houses we would expect to have been built for the richest elements in society. The construction of the ostentatious public buildings that graced early Antonine Verulamium would have been organised, and probably largely financed, by wealthy local dignitaries. It was they who, with government encouragement, fostered pride in the tribal or *civitas* capital, and advertised their own importance by endowing it publicly. It was also members of this elite who undertook the main civic duties, serving as *decuriones* on the council in the *civitas* capital. Each year two magistrates were chosen from among the *decuriones*; these annual magistrates and their junior assistants, the *aediles*, managed tribal

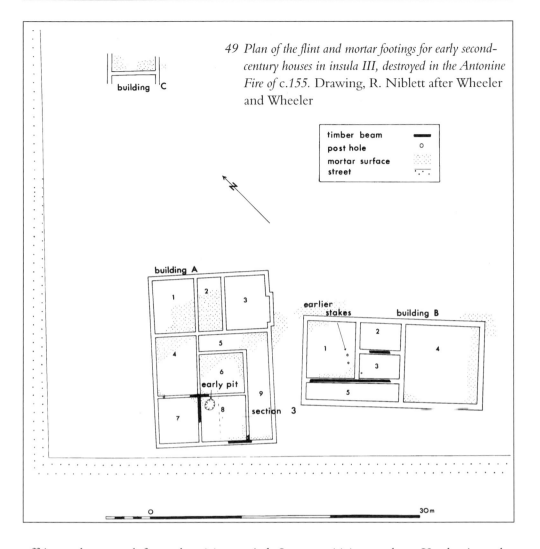

49 Plan of the flint and mortar footings for early second-century houses in insula III, destroyed in the Antonine Fire of c.155. Drawing, R. Niblett after Wheeler and Wheeler

affairs and operated from the *civitas* capital. In a *municipium* such as Verulamium the *decuriones* would technically be required to have houses in the town, but the mid-second-century houses in Verulamium were generally fairly modest buildings. Although members of the social elite may have spent part of their time in the town, on the whole they do not seem to have invested in the construction of luxurious town houses. Instead they expanded their country houses into comfortable villas. A Romano-British villa is by definition a rural site, where the domestic buildings exhibit a high degree of 'Romanisation'. The main residential houses are rectilinear in plan and usually either rested on stone footings, or were completely stone built. They had tiled or stone roofs and hard mortar or tessellated floors. In addition villas show evidence of some degree of comfort and refinement such as plastered and painted walls, heated rooms, or even private bath suites. We know of several country houses in the hinterland of Verulamium which, by the middle of the second century can justifiably be described as villas but which had their origins in the later first century. At Boxmoor House, 8km south-west of Verulamium in the Bulbourne valley, a rectangular timber building was in existence by *c*.75. This has only been partially exposed, and in view of the local practice of constructing rectangular buildings before the conquest, we have to be careful before describing it as a villa at this stage. At Gadebridge, however, a small bathhouse was built, probably towards the end of the first century and certainly well before the construction of the Antonine villa, and here there certainly appears to have been a villa on the site in the late first century. The villas at Gorhambury, Lockleys and Park Street were also established by the late first or early second century.

Of the 16 villas known to have stood within 15km of Verulamium, all those that have been excavated have proved to have been flourishing by the Antonine period. On these sites the main, residential houses were solidly built on flint and mortar footings, with between nine and twelve rooms on the ground floor. The majority were 'winged corridor villas', where the principal rooms were arranged in a rectangular block, with short projecting wings at both ends, and a connecting corridor on one or both sides of the main range. Many incorporated a cellar or basement room, and at least five had bath blocks. Most had painted and plastered walls or ceilings, mortar or tessellated floors, and in some cases the principal rooms had mosaics. The most fully excavated local villa is at Gorhambury, a kilometre west of the town.[6] Here the conquest period 'proto-villa' had continued in use after the conquest, only being replaced in about 75 by another rectangular timber building. This had been burnt down and replaced at the start of the second century by a winged corridor villa with 11 rooms, and a cellar. Apart from the main house the site comprised a small detached bathhouse, two large roundhouses, a masonry tower granary, a smaller rectangular house with corridor, a large 'hall' containing four domestic ovens and a smaller wing room, huts, animal pens, and in the outer enclosure, a strongly built timber storehouse. A formal approach to the main building in the form of a hedge or small avenue suggests that the house may have been fronted by planned gardens. The site's excavators considered the sizeable circular buildings had housed farm workers or were used as store rooms.

None of the other local villas has seen such extensive excavation as was carried out at Gorhambury, so very little is known of their subsidiary buildings, although these certainly existed. At Park Street, 6km south-east of Verulamium, several small rectangular timber buildings were already in existence at the time of the conquest. As at Gorhambury there is little sign of disruption at the time of the conquest, although the 1940s excavations found evidence of burning on the site which was attributed to the Boudiccan revolt. By the early second century a timber building with seven rooms, possibly connected by a corridor, was occupying the site of some of the earlier buildings. By the Antonine period this building had been extended into a winged corridor building with 11 rooms and a detached bathhouse. There is also evidence for several other buildings suggesting a picture similar to that at Gorhambury with at least one and possibly two residential houses, surrounded by smaller buildings housing stores, animals or farm workers.

It used to be thought that there was an absence of villas north of Verulamium. This was probably due more to a lack of fieldwork than any real absence, and it now looks as if the distribution of villas in the area as a whole was very similar to the pattern of occupation in the years immediately before the conquest (**50**). Recently parts of what are almost certainly villas have been recognised at Wheathampstead, Woodcock Hill (Sandridge) and

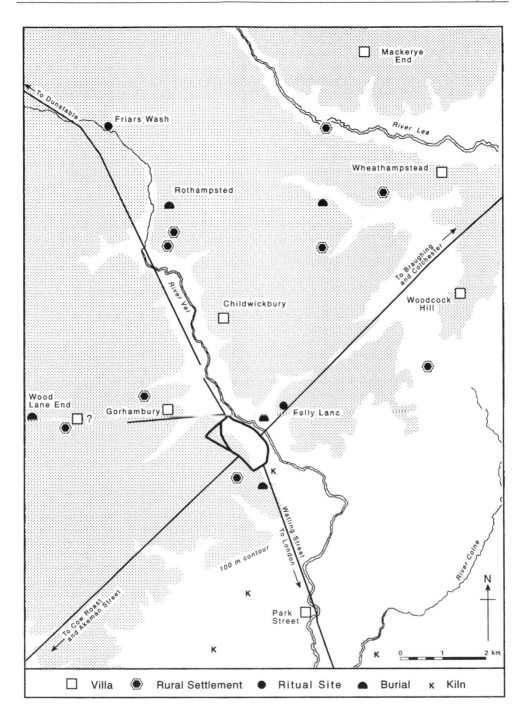

50 Rural settlement in the Verulamium area during the Roman period. Drawn by Phil Dean

Mackerye End. By the early Antonine period villas were springing up along the edge of the Clay with Flints plateau overlooking the valleys of the Lea, Ver, Gade and Bulbourne, just as the late Iron Age farmsteads had done over a century earlier. By contrast the plateau between the river valleys appears empty; presumably here the land was either given over to pasture or was occupied by less successful or fortunate families, scratching a living from less profitable land and with little or no means of building houses substantial enough to be easily discovered today. There is still a notable absence of villas in the area immediately east of Verulamium; indeed evidence for rural settlement here at all is lacking at present. This is almost certainly due to a lack of fieldwork. Much of the area is now built over, or has been disturbed by gravel working, and opportunities for fieldwork are restricted.

Many of the villas developed on, or adjacent to, buildings that were already occupied in the conquest period, and on sites which were continuously occupied from the late Iron Age. Park Street, Gorhambury and Lockleys (south-east of Welwyn) all grew up on sites that were already occupied at the time of the conquest; the same is probably true of the site known only from air photography at Childwickbury, 1.5km north-west of Verulamium (**51**). Wheathampstead, Woodcock Hill and Mackerye End, all sites which have seen only very limited excavation, also appear to have developed on, or immediately adjacent to, sites already occupied in the first half of the first century. It is of course impossible to say whether the second-century occupants of these villas were the descendants of the original settlers, or whether they were newcomers taking over established farms. It is quite possible, however, that the conversion of the late first-century house at Lockleys into a substantial villa in the early years of Antoninus Pius was the work of the great, great grandchildren of the Catuvellaunian farmer who had originally cleared the land at the end of the first century BC.

There are also hints of the continuing influence of native, pre-Roman customs on some of these rural sites. Several of the second-century villas are strikingly bipartite in their plan. In these villas the layout of one part of the main residential building appears closely mirrored by the other. A classic example of this sort of dual layout is provided by the fourth-century villa at Gadebridge.[7] On several other villa sites, for instance Dicket Mead, Park Street and Gorhambury, two separate residential houses were occupied simultaneously; this again could be seen as evidence for dual ownership, either by the owner and his heir, or by two closely related families, one rather wealthier than the other.[8]

Like their houses, funeral monuments of the wealthiest members of society are found, not at Verulamium, but in rural locations. Here again the choice of site tended to be similar to those in the pre-Roman period, with positions on the skyline, overlooking the river valleys, being favourite positions. At Rothamsted, 7km north of Verulamium, a circular, stone built mausoleum with an imposing entrance on the north-east was constructed probably during the reign of the emperor Hadrian.[9] The mausoleum, containing a life-sized statue of a draped figure, stood in the centre of a square walled and ditched burial enclosure. Only a small proportion of this enclosure was uncovered when the site was excavated in 1937; nevertheless two second-century cremation burials were found within it. It is highly likely that many more existed and that this enclosure represents a survival of the tradition of burial within rectilinear enclosures that was so much a feature of the pre-Roman period. Another example of the possible continuity of

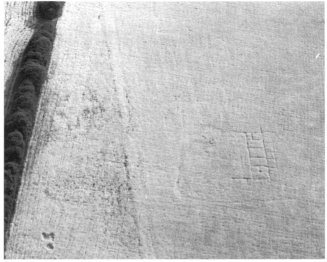

51 Childwickbury villa from the air. The plan of the building may reflect dual occupancy of the house by two separate families, as the two halves appear to be mirror images of each other. The line to the left of the building marks a ditch, possibly part of a pre-Roman enclosure on the site. The site is in private land. Copyright St Albans Museum

existing aristocratic burial traditions is provided by an unusual site at Wood Lane End, 8km south-west of Verulamium.[10] Here a remarkable tower-like mausoleum was constructed towards the end of the first century, on a site overlooking a road leading out of Verulamium towards Akeman Street. The mausoleum was in the form of a Romano-Celtic temple and contained a small, sunken chamber. This had been dug into the past, and no burial or objects were found within it, but it is reminiscent of the sunken funerary chamber associated with the mid-first-century burial at Folly Lane. Contemporary with the Wood Lane End mausoleum was a small bathhouse, presumably used for ritual purification before the performance of whatever commemorative rites were enacted here. Slightly later a second, smaller mausoleum was built 8m south-east of the main structure. This contained a small plinth, rather than a sunken chamber, suggesting that the traditions associated with sunken chambers had died out by the Antonine period.

It seems clear that while willing to endow the tribal capital with expensive buildings, and no doubt to spend a proportion of their time there, the wealthier inhabitants of the area chose to live and die on their country estates. The 16 villas in the Verulamium area all lie within 15km of the town. It is reasonable to assume that the major Roman roads in the area were complemented by an extensive network of trackways; except in mid-winter a family leaving a farm or villa in the Lea or Bulbourne valleys at daybreak, and using ponies and carts, could have reached Verulamium in time to sell their produce in the market or pay their taxes and still return home before dark. It would have been quite feasible even using slower ox-drawn carts.

All this begs the question, who was living in Verulamium? How many of the inhabitants were permanent residents, and what opportunities were open to them to become wealthy? Although never densely built up, nearly all the 40ha in the centre of Verulamium (the area originally bounded by the 1955 ditch) was probably built over at one time or the other in the Roman period. Outside the line of the ditch, the areas enclosed by the Fosse, and later by the town walls, do not appear to have been so densely built over. On the other hand, buildings certainly spread along the main roads here, and although the intervening ground was not necessarily occupied, it was certainly utilised. Who was responsible for all this activity?

Craft and industry in the Roman town

Geophysical surveys by English Heritage in the south and west of the town, outside the line of the 1955 ditch, have suggested the existence of kilns or furnaces close to the town wall in insula XI, while excavations have produced evidence for both metalworking and pottery making within the town. The extent to which industrial activities contributed to Verulamium's prosperity is however a matter of some debate. In the second century enormous quantities of pottery were produced in the Verulamium region. Local kilns produced a range of pots, including flagons and *mortaria* (mixing bowls), jars, beakers, bowls and even amphorae for storing wine and other commodities. The pots were made in a hard, granular fabric, incorporating minute grains of ferrugenous sand and quartz, usually white or buff in colour, but sometimes red or pink according to firing conditions. Coarse, grey wares were also manufactured and used to make storage and cooking jars. The industry had started in the mid-first century when potters began working at Bricket Wood, 4km south of Verulamium.[11] As was a common practice at the time, potters making *mortaria* stamped their wares with their name; in this way the names of two early potters have come down to us, L. Arrius Caludus and Oastrius. Both also included the Romano-British name associated with modern Bricket Wood — Lugdunum. By the start of the second century, pottery was being produced even closer to Verulamium; five kilns have been excavated outside the south gate of Verulamium, and kiln wasters and kiln debris dating from the first half of the second century have been recorded in insulae V and XIII of the town itself. Some of the geophysical anomalies detected in recent surveys may prove to be pottery kilns (**52**). Far from being confined to Verulamium and its immediate outskirts however, pottery kilns were strung out along Watling Street, over much of the area between Verulamium and Brockley Hill just outside modern Stanmore. At Brockley Hill itself more than 20 kilns have been recorded. The site lies on Watling Street, almost exactly midway between Verulamium and London. A Roman settlement has been known to exist here since the sixteenth century and it has been identified as *Salonicae,* mentioned in the late Roman compilation of routes known as the Antonine Itinerary. The name suggests that the place developed from a private estate owned by Salonicus. There is little to suggest that Verulamium itself was the centre of the pottery industry. Instead the siting of kilns seems to have been determined more by the presence of Watling Street and the ease with which products could been transported to London. The remains of what appears to be a wharf at Park Street reminds us of the possibility that the Ver and Colne were navigable by barge; this would have provided an ideal method of transporting both pottery and tiles to London.[12] In other words, the pottery industry is likely to have contributed to the wealth of entrepreneurs or people who were lucky enough to occupy land close to Watling Street and with suitable clay deposits, rather than to the town itself. The kiln owners may have chosen to invest their wealth in the town, but the town itself was not the industrial centre and they usually operated outside it. It is interesting in this context

52 The floor of an early second-century pottery kiln in Verulam Hills Field during excavation in 1968. The edge of the stokehole can be seen in the left-hand corner, but no trace of the superstructure survived. Copyright St Albans Museum

that Oastrius stamped his wares as made in Lugdunum (presumably the name of his estate) not Verulamium which lay only 4km to the north.

The Verulamium region pottery industry reached its peak in the first half of the second century when its products flooded the London market and supplied forts on Hadrian's Wall. By the later second century the industry had declined dramatically. Even in areas close to home, such as the small rural settlement at Foxholes Farm, near Hertford, most of the coarse pottery used in the third and fourth centuries came from Hadham in east Hertfordshire, or from kilns in the Oxford region, rather than from Verulamium. A small number of kilns in the Verulamium region clearly continued to operate throughout the third and fourth centuries, but they produced only sufficient coarse, grey wares to supply a restricted local area with cooking pots and storage jars. Even here the bulk of pottery was imported from further afield.

The other industrial activity that has left traces in Verulamium is metalworking. The importance of the iron deposits in the Bulbourne valley has already been commented on, and traces of iron-making have been found in the Berkhamsted area from the early first century. Stuart Bryant, in unpublished research, has suggested that by the end of the Iron Age the area around Berkhamsted was one of the major iron smelting areas in the south-east, and coin evidence from Cow Roast suggests that this industry continued to flourish until the end of the second century. At both Gadebridge and Boxmoor villas there were signs that iron smelting was taking place prior to and during the lives of the villas, and it seems reasonable to assume that the initial smelting was generally carried out close to the deposits of ore, rather than in Verulamium which would have entailed transporting large quantities of heavy and bulky material.

There are, however, numerous references in excavation reports to evidence for metalworking in Verulamium itself. The evidence for blacksmithing in Verulamium is predominantly in the form of small hearths or bowl furnaces in which the raw, semi-worked blooms were heated and prepared, before being forged into finished articles (**53**). To what extent these smiths were simply servicing the wants of particular families and neighbours, and to what extent they were part of a larger industry, is difficult to say. We should also not forget the possibility that much small-scale metalworking, particularly the repair and reworking of old or broken equipment, may have been carried out by itinerant smiths, visiting the town periodically. Conversely some smiths, based in Verulamium, may have spent much of their time travelling round the rural area.

There is ample evidence from Verulamium for bronze working from the mid-first century onwards. The evidence for this is largely in the form of bronze-working slag, crucibles and scrap metal in what were clearly workshops. As will be discussed below, the inhabitants of Verulamium were able to obtain bronzes of the highest quality. Some of the finest of these were no doubt imported, but finds such as the crucibles used for enamelling, or those containing traces of gold that were found in a storeroom behind one of the houses fronting onto Watling Street in insula XIV, suggest that demands for fine jewellery were met by local supply. In the same buildings the tubs or boxes placed beneath workbenches in order to collect the shavings from the manufacture of lathe-turned bronze vessels on the bench above, tell a similar story.[13]

While the production of bronze vessels and jewellery demands specialists, we cannot be certain that these professional metalworkers were permanently resident either in Verulamium or on the villas. Quite apart from metalsmiths, the whole question of itinerant and seasonal working has never been addressed. Many occupations may have been seasonal with substantial elements in the population moving between two or more different bases. The movement of stock between summer and winter pasture along with shepherds and cowhands is an obvious example, but other occupations may also have been conducted seasonally. The iron industry particularly would have required large quantities of charcoal and it is quite possible that some of the small settlements in the Chilterns above Berkhamsted were occupied by charcoal burners and used for only part of the year. Elsewhere the pottery kilns may not have operated throughout the year. The drying of unfired vessels to reach a leather-hard consistency would require reasonable climatic conditions without the extremes of heat and cold, and so may not have been feasible during the winter or in the height of summer. At these periods the workers were presumably employed elsewhere.

Verulamium must have been the site of the regular markets essential to any agricultural society. Here surplus agricultural produce would be exchanged for goods not readily available on farmsteads in the Chilterns. The agricultural regimes in the Roman period differed little from those of the late Iron Age, although there seems to have been a gradual shift from a predominantly pastoral economy to one of mixed farming. Nevertheless, animal husbandry remained important throughout the Roman period, and periodic cattle, sheep and horse markets would have been essential to maintain the stock. From the late first until the early fifth centuries a wide area, stretching from the Basilica to the river, was maintained as an open gravelled space. When first laid out this may have covered the whole width of insula XIX, forming an open area in front of the Basilica. By the second half of the second century, however, houses were being built along its northern side leaving a 30m

53 Remains of a late first-century smithy in insula XIX during excavation in 1987; the pear-shaped area of burning in the centre of the photograph represents burning in the base of a small bowl furnace. Copyright St Albans Museum

wide piazza, covering nearly 4000m² outside the north-east entrance into the Basilica (shown on figure **35**). It is possible this piazza was used as a supplementary market place, perhaps for livestock for which the Forum itself may not have been suitable. It is worth noting the presence of a similar open space alongside the Basilica at Cirencester.

There is a certain amount of evidence for the sale of meat in Verulamium. *Macella* tended to be used as meat markets, although this was not invariably the case, as is shown by the variety of commodities represented on the mosaics in the *macellum* at Ostia, a short distance outside Rome. At Verulamium the *macellum* was first built in timber shortly after the Boudiccan revolt. After being destroyed in the Antonine fire it was rebuilt in masonry, and continued in use until the very end of the Roman period. Comparatively little material was found within it when it was excavated in 1938, but fieldwalking since has recovered quantities of cattle bone and teeth in this area, while a watching brief on a pipe line trench approximately 120m to the north recorded an enormous dump of animal (mainly cattle) bone in a Roman rubbish pit just outside the town wall. That cattle were being butchered in third-century Verulamium on a commercial scale was demonstrated by the tips of cattle bone in the upper filling of a pit on the Folly Lane/Oysterfield site. The tips contained bones from the hindquarters of 37 cattle, all showing signs of intensive butchery typical of large-scale meat processing.[14]

The by-products of butchery on this scale would themselves have been used for a variety of processes. Principal among these would have been leather-working. As yet evidence for leather-working in Verulamium is confined to the discarded shoes and leather off-cuts found in the later first–century filling of the Central Enclosure ditch in insula XIII. It is possible, however, that some of the pits containing cess at the Folly Lane/Oysterfield site were used in the tanning process. Apart from suggestions of bone working in an early Antonine workshop in insula XIII, there is surprisingly little evidence for this industry in Verulamium, and other related processes, such as glue and tallow production, have left no traces at all, although it is safe to assume that these were carried out alongside leather-working.

Little work has as yet been undertaken on the collections of animal bone from Verulamium, but such evidence as is available suggests that beef was the principal meat consumed throughout the Roman period. This is reflected on the surrounding villa sites where the proportion of sheep in the diet generally declines in the course of the Roman period, although there is some evidence for an increase in sheep on a few villa sites in the fourth century. The majority of remains found, however, are those of older animals who are more likely to have been kept for their wool rather than as a source of food. Parts of three iron wool-carding combs from Verulamium or its immediate hinterland represent something of a concentration of these tools, while the mortar lined 'tanks' recorded by the Wheelers in two late Roman town houses could have been used for fulling cloth. The organisation of the local woollen industry however is far from clear, and the needs of many families were probably met in the home. Two iron strigils found in a rich late first-century grave had been wrapped in pieces of cloth (**colour plate 9**), the impressions of which were preserved in the corrosion on the strigils. At least two different fabrics were represented. One was well spun and carefully woven, the other was much coarser with striking variations in the thickness of the thread, and showing numerous mistakes in the weaving, suggesting a cloth produced by a non-professional weaver using home-spun wool.[15]

Pork was evidently consumed at all periods but was secondary in importance to beef and mutton. Pork consumption may have been a mark of higher social status; the wealthy late-Roman villa at Dicket Mead in the Mimram valley 15km north-east of Verulamium produced unusually large numbers of pig bones, many of them from young animals, suggesting that sucking pig was eaten here fairly frequently. A similar picture is presented by the animal bones from the villa site at Gorhambury. Rubbish dumped in a cellar on another probable villa site at Woodcock Hill (Sandridge) in the later second century contained comparatively large numbers of (probably wild) boar. Although no doubt the meat was eaten, the bones must represent hunting, probably carried out primarily as a sport by men of higher status.[16] Hunting generally does not appear to have supplied a significant element in the diet, especially so in Verulamium although there is some evidence for an increase in the consumption of venison in the late Roman period on villas at Dicket Mead, 12km north of Verulamium, and at Chorleywood[17] 20km to the south.

A number of so-called corn-drying ovens have been recorded from Verulamium or its immediate surroundings, raising the question of the extent to which grain was processed in the town. The construction of a granary at the Gorhambury villa in the second century, capable of storing 88,000lb (39,900kg) of grain, implies that a considerable area around Verulamium was under arable cultivation. Inside the town three small granaries were destroyed in the early Antonine fire, all of them in insula XIII; in the third century what may be a tower granary was built in the west corner of insula II, building 1.[18] Very little environmental analysis has been carried out from the Verulamium area, but the burnt grain in the insula XIII granaries was overwhelmingly spelt wheat, with a small proportion of emmer wheat. This picture is in line with the composition of surviving deposits from the villas. The grain in insula XIII had all been processed by the time it was stored here and included no weed seeds or chaff. By contrast, burnt grain from the presumed villa sites at Woodcock Hill and Mackerye End included substantial proportions of chaff and weed seeds, implying that threshing (and presumably any preliminary drying) was carried out in the country before the processed grain was transported to Verulamium.[19] In 1968 substantial Roman foundations were found close to the river Ver, 600m east of the London Gate. These were tentatively interpreted as the remains of a mill, but they were only recorded in the course of road works and it is difficult to interpret the resulting plan as that of a mill with any confidence. Nevertheless, the presence of a sizeable Roman building so close to the river is, to say the least, suggestive. Grain for most domestic purposes, however, must have been ground on small, hand-turned querns, numerous fragments of which survive.

Most of the grain contained in one of the granaries in insula XIII was already sprouting when burnt. This may have simply been due to inefficient storage, but it is perhaps more likely that it was about to be used to make beer. Beer was drunk extensively in the Roman Empire, particularly in the western provinces, and 'Celtic' beer was one of the products listed in the emperor Diocletian's price-fixing edict in the early fourth century. Many of the so-called corn-drying ovens from Verulamium may have been used for gently heating wheat or barley as part of the brewing process. Some of the large hearths from the town should probably also be seen in terms of brewing. It has already been suggested that the large hearth in the yard of the Antonine house in the south-east corner of insula XIII was used in a process that also required a ready supply of water as well as wheat and the premises may well have belonged to a brewer. The numerous bread ovens in the same building are easily explained in the light of Pliny's remark that the Celts used the barm (foam produced by the initial steeping of the wheat in water during brewing) as a leaven for bread.[20] A similar but slightly earlier hearth was excavated in 1930 by the Wheelers in insula I. It too lay just outside the contemporary building, and was 2m long and incorporated a raised floor with two underlying flues supported by a solid foundation.[21]

It is difficult to say to what extent people living within Verulamium farmed the surrounding countryside themselves. Aerial photography in the 1970s over Jersey Farm (3.5km north-east of Verulamium) and on the line of the M25 near Chiswell Green (3km to the south) revealed areas covered by trackways and small square or rectangular fields delimited by ditches and each covering about 1.5-2ha. The date of these fields is uncertain, but they may well belong to the late Iron Age or Romano-British period. Whether they were cultivated by people living in Verulamium, or whether they were associated with as yet unrecognised settlements nearer at hand, are also questions to which there is no answer. However, the short lengths of ditches visible on air photographs just outside the north-west (Chester) Gate may be boundaries for allotments worked by families living in the town itself. These ditches include the 'undated' earthworks shown west of the town on figure **19**. South of these ditches the pre-Roman farmstead at Prae Wood ceased to be occupied after the later first century, but there is no reason to suppose that the associated paddocks and droveways were abandoned and the area was quite probably farmed by someone living inside the town boundary. Apart from Prae Wood the only other pre-

Roman site immediately adjacent to Verulamium that has seen any archaeological recording is that at Mayne Avenue (**19**). Here a large aisled building was put up resting on flint and mortar footings; a late-Roman corn-drying oven was also recorded nearby. This is in essence a rural site, but it lay within a few metres of the town and appears to have been occupied for most of the Roman period, and like the Prae Wood paddocks was probably farmed by someone living in the town. The small number of agricultural implements that have been recorded from within Verulamium itself includes an iron plough-share, but most are tools suited more to market gardening than farming, such as iron tips for wooden spades or prongs from wooden rakes. While some inhabitants of the town doubtless worked nearby small-holdings, many must have kept hens, goats or pigs in plots within the town, where they probably also grew vegetables for domestic use. Although most of the central area of Verulamium was built over at some time or other in the Roman period, there always seems to have been substantial areas of open ground. It is reasonable to assume that many of these areas were used for gardens, paddocks or orchards.

A question that is often asked, but which is impossible to answer fully, is how many people actually lived in Verulamium during the Roman period. Obviously the population varied in the course of the Roman period. In spite of Tacitus's figure of 70,000 Romans and their sympathisers killed in Verulamium, Colchester and London during the Boudiccan revolt, it is difficult to imagine more than about 1000 inhabitants at the most in Boudiccan Verulamium. Tacitus' figures were probably exaggerated and included those killed during the final battle against Boudicca, as well (no doubt) as the population of rural areas surrounding the towns. However, there is no unequivocal evidence for destruction on either the Park Street or the Gorhambury villa sites at this period. A century later the population of the Roman town may have risen to nearer 5000 and at certain times of year this figure could have been doubled with the addition of seasonal residents and itinerant workers. At times of festivals and major markets Verulamium may have been packed; at other times it may have appeared half-empty.

Verulamium as a market and administrative centre

Throughout its life Verulamium must, above all, have provided the market for the surrounding district. Here any surplus from the local villas and the humbler, but more numerous, rural settlements could be exchanged for essential and luxury goods. London must also have provided an important market for the whole Verulamium region. Watling Street gave a quick and easy route to what, at least in the later first and second centuries, was a major trading centre; produce brought to Verulamium could be rapidly carted to London. At the same time, imported goods coming into London could be easily transported to Verulamium, as the quantities of samian ware and other fine tableware from Gaul indicate. Numerous other commodities were also carted along Watling Street. Amphorae for wine, fish sauce and olive oil from Spain and Italy appear at Verulamium as early as the first century, and by the end of the century a flood of imported objects was entering the town, including small everyday articles such as the bronze brush holder recently found in an early second-century context at Woodcock Hill. This was stamped as being made in the workshop of Agathangelus, a smith working in the central Alps in the mid-first century.

Verulamium would have combined its role as a market with that of the local administrative centre and tribal capital of the Catuvellauni. Like most of the British tribes, the tribal identity of the Catuvellauni continued throughout the Roman period; in the later fourth century the Catuvellauni were still called upon to perform state duties, in this case by contributing to the repair of a milecastle on Hadrian's Wall. As the main administrative capital for the Catuvellauni, people would have had to come to Verulamium for particular, but essential, reasons. The Basilica at Verulamium was the place where legal transactions were conducted and justice administered. Most lawsuits not involving an appeal to the emperor (a right reserved to Roman citizens), would be dealt with here. Verulamium was also the place where taxes were assessed and records maintained. Apart from levies in kind, taxes would have been paid for in gold. Farmers from the surrounding area must have had to exchange agricultural surpluses in the market in order to accumulate sufficient coinage to pay their tax. They would then have had to visit a moneychanger (probably in the Forum) in order to exchange the bronze coins used for the majority of everyday transactions for the necessary gold coins.

It is also important not to overlook the importance of the town as a centre for local organisations, traces of which are not readily recognisable in the archaeological record. A third-century beaker from a grave in Dunstable was dedicated by the guild of *dendrophori* of Verulamium. *Dendrophori* were priests in the cult of the eastern mother goddess Cybele. Among other attributes, Cybele was patron of woodworkers. It would not be stretching the evidence unduly to suggest that the grave was that of a carpenter or timber merchant who had lived in Dunstable but was a member of a religious organisation based in Verulamium, ten miles south-east along Watling Street. One or two large buildings known from aerial photographs may have been used as guild headquarters. They stood on the south side of Watling Street in insula XXXIV. The western building is clearest on photographs and consisted of a large square court or hall behind two pairs of rooms, separated by a corridor leading to the street (**colour plate 22**).

Verulamium as a religious centre

At least seven temples are known within Verulamium itself while two (possibly three) lay a short distance outside the town walls. Of those within the town, one stood in the centre of the south-west side of the Forum, and was probably dedicated to Rome and the imperial cult; it was rebuilt after the Antonine fire and at the same time another temple was added to the west corner of the Forum. These two are the only classical temples in the town. They stood on raised *podia* approached by steps from the Forum court and would have consisted of a rectangular shrine or *cella* surrounded by a portico, with a triangular pediment facing towards the Forum court (**54**). Apart from a rectangular shrine with an apsidal western end, that stood just outside the London Gate, all the other temples in Verulamium were of the Romano-Celtic type, with a central shrine or *cella*, surrounded by a portico or verandah. Three, two in insula XVII and one in insula XXI, are known only from air photos and geophysics, but the large temple in insula XVI behind the theatre, and the triangular temple in insula VII, were excavated in the 1930s. Both were first built in the later first century, but concentrations of early coins and brooches on both sites suggest that they stood in positions that were already sacred in the mid-first century. An

54 Part of a ceramic model of a classical temple showing five columns with decorated capitals. The model was probably part of a small domestic shrine. Found in later Roman contexts in insula XIII. Maximum width 18.5cm. Copyright St Albans Museum

eighteenth–century record by Joshua Webster of what appears to be a Roman altar may mark the site of another temple. It was found a short distance to the south-east of the Silchester Gate. More recently this same area has produced two fine bronze statuettes (**colour plates 14-15**). It is also adjacent to the Roman site that replaced the King Harry Lane cemetery, and produced pipe clay figurines of 'mother goddesses', a 'votive' model axe, decorative bronze plaques and a large number of Romano-British brooches. Such a concentration of possibly votive material suggests the presence of a temple nearby.

The triangular temple is so called because of its unusual plan. Its position, at the point at which Watling Street entered the late first-century town from the south-east, meant that it occupied an awkwardly shaped plot between the oblique line of Watling Street and that of the main street grid. It had the advantage that anyone entering the town from London was immediately confronted by the temple façade, and the altar in front of it, but it also forced a modification of the normal Romano-Celtic plan. Instead of occupying a central position within the portico, the *cella* and two flanking shrines had to be placed against the north wall. The suggestion that the temple was dedicated to Cybele is based on the discovery in what must have been votive pits in the temple court, of burnt seeds and scales from pinecones of the Italian pine (*pinus pinea*). The pine figured in the rituals associated with the worship of Cybele and her consort Attis but the Italian pine is not a species that occurs naturally in Britain; either the cones, or a tree itself, must have been imported. Cybele was a mother-goddess whose worship originated in the Near East but among her attributes was that of a guardian of cities, a role which would explain her presence here at the entrance to Verulamium.

The large Romano-Celtic temple in insula XVI also stood in a walled precinct. The precinct opened onto the Verulamium theatre in insula XV, and the two were obviously closely linked. The theatre was first built in about 140. Its southern side overlay remains of an early second-century building, but as Sheppard Frere showed by excavation in the 1950s, most of the site had been maintained as an open, gravelled space since the mid-first century. Presumably this space was used for events that later took place in the theatre.

Together the insula XVI temple and the theatre covered an area of 12,000m², or 15,000m² if the precinct area extended west into insula XXXI where air photographs have revealed what appears to be the wall of a large court. Even so the temple and theatre were only a part of a much larger religious area that extended outside the town boundary and across the river.

The focus of this extensive area was the site of the mid-first-century royal burial on the Folly Lane site. At some time, probably late in the first century, a large Romano-Celtic temple had been built on the site of the original funeral pyre, which up until then had been marked by a standing post. The temple faced towards the turf stack over the burial and funerary shaft. The ditch surrounding the enclosure in which the burial lay had been kept clean and clear of rubbish ever since it was first dug a century earlier. In about 140-150, however, it was deliberately filled in and its line carefully marked out by a band of chalk, so as to be clearly visible from the town below. At about the same time a large number of deep pits or shafts began to be dug on the lower slope of the Oysterfields hillside below the entrance into the Folly Lane enclosure. Several of these pits contained votive deposits; in some cases fragments of face jars, with the moulded faces of the sides of the jars carefully cut away, had been thrown into the half-filled pit. Other pits contained horse or ox skulls, and in the base of one third-century example was the skull of a young man who had been killed by a blow to the head and decapitated; the flesh had then been cut away, both from the scalp and from the face. The mid-second century also saw the construction of a large bathhouse, close to a small stream 500m south of the Folly Lane temple. The baths, comparable in size to the town baths at Silchester, were well appointed and capable of accommodating a large number of people (**55-6**). They faced away from Verulamium and towards the Folly Lane/Oysterfields site, and were clearly associated with it rather than with the town. The excavator, Chris Saunders, was of the opinion that they may only have been used seasonally, presumably at times of festival associated with the temple.

The whole complex was linked by road to the theatre and insula XVI temple on the other side of the river (*see* **34**, AD 150). Presumably this road was used as some sort of processional way. While the baths were probably used for ceremonial purification, the road would allow devotees to witness whatever events took place in the theatre and to process ceremonially to the Folly Lane temple.

The close association between the Folly Lane temple and burial demonstrates that the cult here was originally focused on a hero or ancestor cult. By the mid-second century, however, it may also have become associated with other cults. It could well have been associated with a local tribal god or gods, while a tiny bronze model of an owl from the site may be evidence for the worship of Minerva, one of whose attributes was an owl. Minerva's brother Mercury was obviously worshipped extensively in Verulamium as the discovery of three bronze statuettes in the town demonstrates. One of Mercury's roles was as patron of markets, and so his worship would have been particularly appropriate here. A cult venerating the head is a well-known aspect of late Iron Age religion, and there are suggestions that it persisted into later periods; certainly the skulls and face pots in some of the shafts imply that it was observed in second- and third-century Verulamium. The Folly Lane/Oysterfield pits may also have been connected with a well or water cult, and indeed

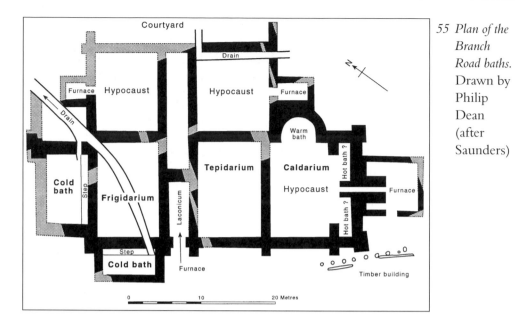

55 Plan of the Branch Road baths. Drawn by Philip Dean (after Saunders)

the whole Ver valley from Verulamium to the river's source 8km to the north-west may have had a religious significance to the local population. In 1957 a sizeable collection of small Romano-British objects, including later Roman coins and two pewter plates, were found in the bed of the Ver and interpreted as votive offerings thrown into the river. Small brooches, representing a warrior or horseman god, may represent similar offerings thrown into the marsh from the first-century causeway outside the 'Timber Tower'. This same deposit produced a magnificent bronze skillet (**colour plate 13**) and the tiny model of the dinner party guest (or river deity) shown on figure **42**; both could well be offerings to a local water deity. Further evidence for a river or water cult is provided by the discovery of two Romano-Celtic temples close to the source of the Ver near Friars Wash (**57**). The presence of a triple dyke adjacent to the temples may be an indication that the site was already sacred in the early first century, and during the Roman period it may have marked the limit of the Verulamium *territorium*.

With this plethora of evidence for different cults at Verulamium it is not difficult to imagine large numbers of people being drawn from the surrounding countryside to Verulamium for seasonal festivals based around the river, the Folly Lane and insula XVI temples and in the theatre. Such festivals were no doubt accompanied by important fairs and markets.

The late second and third centuries

Neither the Folly Lane/Oysterfield site, nor the Insula XVI temple/theatre complex seem to have been affected by the Antonine fire. Nevertheless this ravaged large areas of the lower part of Verulamium and it is now becoming clear that in some badly affected places recovery was delayed for 50 years or longer.

There is at present an apparent dearth of shops and workshops dating from the late second and early third centuries. Although workshops in insula XVIII appear to have been rebuilt shortly after the fire, the brewing and metalworking enterprises carried on in the south-east corner of insula XIII were not revived before the very end of the second century, while the row of workshops along Watling Street in insula XIV was not rebuilt for over a century.

Among the buildings destroyed in the Antonine fire was the Forum/Basilica complex. Excavations on the west corner of the Forum and the east corner of the Basilica, by Wheeler and Corder respectively, demonstrated that

56 The base of the hypocaust in a hot room in the second-century baths at Branch Road. Copyright St Albans Museum

the complex had been rebuilt from ground level sometime after the third quarter of the second century. Unfortunately the modest amount of material found in both excavations makes precise dating impossible and while we might assume that the Forum/Basilica would have represented a priority for rebuilding it is worth remembering that the second-century Basilica at the Atrebates' capital at Silchester may have remained uncompleted for more than a century.[22] At Verulamium the plan of the rebuilt Forum/Basilica is not yet fully understood. Although it followed lines that were basically similar to those of its predecessor, the rooms flanking the central nave of the Basilica were now much larger, while the Forum acquired an additional temple at its west corner and the previously open portico surrounding the Forum court was bricked up. The Forum court itself may now have been somewhat narrower. As in the earlier version, the post-Antonine Forum/Basilica incorporated a substantial amount of dressed Barnack stone, and it is possible that this is the source of the short columns in the same stone that were subsequently incorporated into the tower of the eleventh-century Abbey (**colour plate 2**). They could have come from a clerestory in the Roman Basilica.

At least one major building in the town centre lay in ruins for nearly 50 years. This was the bath building in the north corner of insula III. It was not until the early years of the third century that the burnt rubble from the building, including heavily burnt flue tiles, *tubuli linguli* from the vaulted roof, and fragments of decorative Purbeck marble was shovelled away and the new baths laid out. Like that of the earlier building, little has yet

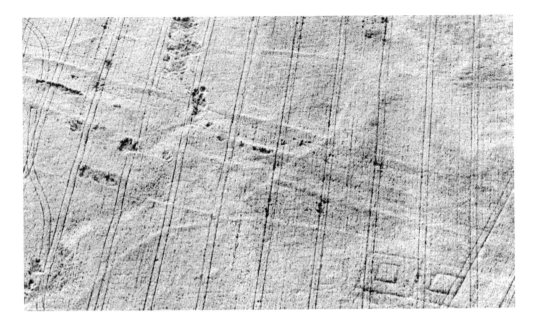

57 Romano-Celtic temples near Friars Wash with traces of a triple dyke adjacent to them. The dyke may well date from the pre-Roman period. Copyright St Albans Museum

been revealed of the plan, but it incorporated massive vaulted masonry drains, a hypocaust and a range of small rooms or shops along the street on the north of the building. North of the Forum the *macellum* had also been destroyed in the fire, but this was rebuilt more promptly. While less than two thirds the size of its predecessor, the late second-century *macellum* was a masonry building of considerable pretension. A wide gate, opposite the theatre on the other side of Watling Street, opened onto a court surrounded by a large masonry drain and flanked by two ranges of shops. At the north-east end of the court, facing the entrance from Watling Street was a raised, stone-built apse. This may once have housed a large statue, perhaps that of the presiding deity; in this case Mercury, patron of markets, would have been particularly appropriate (**58**).

The earlier aqueduct that had supplied the *macellum* from the north no longer operated after the Antonine fire, and this may have been the time when the town was provided with a new water supply. Recent air photographs have revealed a possible leat or aqueduct leaving the river Ver 2.8km north of Verulamium. On the photographs its course can be traced intermittently in the direction of the Chester Gate. It appears to follow the natural contours, and allows a gradual fall of 14.5m over its 2.8km length (**59**). It was only recognised in 1995 and at the time of writing it has not been possible to confirm it by excavation. It is still possible that it is not Roman at all, but was cut to serve the medieval nunnery of St Mary de Pre that lay on Watling Street a short distance outside Verulamium; on the other hand it is perhaps more likely that it served the conduit bringing water into Verulamium along the south-west side of Watling Street and excavated by Frere in the footings of the northern monumental arch.

58 The Macellum
as it may have
appeared in the
second century.
Drawn by
Phil Dean

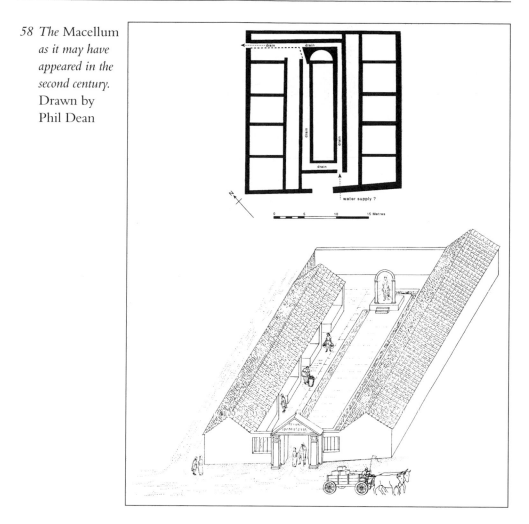

Replacing public buildings and providing a new water supply suggests that there were substantial resources available, and certainly there is evidence for very considerable wealth in the town in the later second and third centuries. This is particularly evident in areas that were not so severely affected by the fire, but by the early third century widespread building, especially of private houses, seems to have been going on in most parts of the town. Most of the 23 houses excavated by the Wheelers in the south of the town in the 1930s were built at the end of the second century or early in the third, although some replaced smaller, earlier buildings (**60**).[23] In insulae **XX-XXII** and **XXVIII** Sheppard Frere excavated parts of four houses that were all constructed in the late second century or during the first half of the third.[24] Most of the buildings known only from air photography also probably date from after the mid-second century. It was only after the Antonine fire, and perhaps as a direct result of it, that significant numbers of private houses were built with flint and mortar footings, even though this type of foundation had been used for public buildings since the late first century. Since only buildings with stone or mortar foundations are visible from the air, it follows that most of the buildings we see on the photographs probably

59 *Air photograph showing the possible aqueduct in private land a short distance west of Verulamium. A former river course can be seen in the foreground as a dark, winding band; the aqueduct takes a wide curve before entering the town near the top left hand corner of the photograph. Other marks represent later field drains Watling Street, and the medieval priory of St Mary de Pre.* Copyright St Albans Museum

belong to this later period of Verulamium's history. As in earlier periods, private houses show considerable variation in plan and size, ranging from simple strip buildings to large mansions with ranges of rooms extending along two or three sides of courtyards or gardens. Only one house is known with a fully enclosed courtyard. This lies in the west corner of insula III, next door to the public baths. It replaced three small town houses destroyed in the Antonine fire, and contained 23 rooms on the ground floor alone. It is possible that it was the town *mansio*, an official 'guest house' designed to accommodate officials and couriers on government service. At least two officials lost small personal belongings in Verulamium. One, a small bronze model of a ceremonial sword, was found in insula XIV and the other, a fine bronze cruciform brooch, had been lost in the insula III courtyard house itself. Both are items which have been associated with high-ranking officers (**61 & 69**). Other buildings, however, have an equally strong claim to be the Verulamium *mansio*. One is a large building in the centre of insula XXXVII which seems to have included its own bath block (**colour plate 22**). In fact there are at least 14 houses from the town with 12 or more ground floor rooms, thus providing comparable accommodation to that of the Antonine villas in the surrounding countryside. It is clear that late second- and early third-century Verulamium was a place of considerable affluence. Forty-one mosaic floors have been recorded from the town since the eighteenth century. Many of these have now either been destroyed or survive in such small fragments as to be impossible to date. At least 16 however were laid in the later second century, and 9 of the 15 hypocausts known from private houses in the town are of similar date (**colour plate 17**).

60 A fine geometric mosaic in building 8, insula IV during excavation in 1932. The stokehole for a hypocaust appears in the foreground. Reproduced courtesy of the St Albans Museum, copyright reserved

An unusual quantity of painted wall plaster survives from the town, much of it currently displayed in the Verulamium Museum. Among the best preserved is the painted wall and ceiling from a winged corridor house in insula XXI (building 2). The range of rooms along the street frontage had been destroyed by the hollow-way that was the lane up Bluehouse Hill prior to the construction of the modern A4145, but Sheppard Frere's excavation of the surviving parts of the house, and particularly its south-west wing, have given us a unique picture of the sophisticated internal decoration of a wealthy house in Verulamium in the final years of the second century. The south-west wing evidently comprised the principal 'public rooms' of the house. The rooms, of various lengths, were over 4m wide and were served by a corridor running around three sides of a courtyard. The corridor had a plain red tessellated floor and a plastered ceiling, painted reddish purple and with a pattern of octagonal panels separated by yellow wheat stalks. Within each panel was a grey dove or a leopard's or panther's mask (**colour plate 18**). The walls of the corridor were over 3m high and had also been plastered and painted. At the base of the wall was a dado painted to imitate marble panels. Above this the main area of wall was similarly divided into panels, painted red and framed by yellow candelabra supporting floral swags. At the centre of each panel was a dove (**colour plate 19**). The top portion of the wall had been decorated with a red frieze with a darker scroll pattern, but plaster from

this part of the wall was badly preserved and the details of the design are unclear. At its south-east end the corridor led to a small room, possibly an entrance lobby opening into the garden. The corridor ceiling here was red rather than purple and may have included human masks in the design as well as birds. The entrance room itself had a tessellated floor and dark green painted wall plaster; along the base of the wall was a pink, grey and cream coloured dado. On the other side of the corridor, opposite the entrance room was one of the main rooms of the house. Measuring 7.4 x 4.4m, it contained a high quality mosaic, exceptionally well preserved and depicting a lion carrying a stag's head in his mouth (**colour plate 21**). In this room the predominant wall colour was emerald green, although here again the wall had been divided into panels, in this case defined by red bands. At the top of the wall was a painted moulded cornice, and another probably separated the main expanse of the wall from the painted dado at its base. The decoration of the dado itself seems to have varied in different parts of the room. On the south-west wall it was a simple dark red, but on the adjacent wall it had a Greek key pattern painted in black on a yellow background and divided into panels by red lines. The walls of the room, which are estimated to have been about 5m high, would have risen above the roof level of the corridor and allowed clerestory windows to provide lighting; chalk voussoirs from the arches of these windows were found in the rubble among the fallen plaster. The external wall of the corridor in this wing of the house had also been plastered and painted. A large fragment from the frieze was found lying face down in the courtyard. It had been painted with a particularly attractive design of alternating pheasants and panther or leopard masks, enclosed by a running 'acanthus' scroll (**colour plate 20**). Although to modern taste the colour schemes in at least some of the rooms may seem bizarre, the techniques and designs employed are comparable to some of the best in the western provinces of the Empire. The painting of the doves and pheasants in particular is the work of a skilled professional.

Because excavations have uncovered very few complete house plans of this date we still know little about how various rooms or ranges of rooms were used, while as at other periods our understanding of the paddocks, working yards, gardens and out-buildings that must have been associated with so many houses is still minimal. The different uses to which different parts of a house might be put are illustrated by one

61 Bronze model of a ceremonial sword found near Watling Street in insula XIV. Overall length 7.8cm. Copyright St Albans Museum

of the few houses to be fully excavated in Verulamium since the 1930s. This is building 1 in insula XXVIII. Like parts of insulae III and XIII, the south corner of this insula had lain empty for 50 years after the Antonine fire, in spite of its central position opposite one of the entrances into the Forum. Early in the third century however the site was levelled and a large house constructed around three sides of a gravelled courtyard. On the north-west side of the courtyard was a winged corridor house, with a central range of four rooms (one of them possibly a stairwell). The rooms were flanked by corridors or verandahs and there were two small projecting rooms at the ends of both corridors. The house contained three hypocausts and can easily be seen as a small, but well-appointed and comfortable domestic house. The rooms in the north-east wing of the complex, however, suggest a rather different picture. They included a large public latrine, fronting onto the street along the north-west side of the Forum. The latrine was housed in a room over 6m long with timber seats arranged over a large tiled drain running centrally across the room and of one build with the masonry sewer that ran alongside the street. That the latrine was a successful commercial enterprise is suggested by the subsequent addition of a second, two-seater latrine in the north-east corner of the same building. In the meantime a large room between the two latrines was used for some kind of commercial or industrial process involving the disposal of large quantities of water since it too was provided with a drain leading into the sewer along the street. Another remarkable feature of the north-east range was a large underground chamber, L-shaped in plan, with two arms, each 19m long and just under 2.5m wide. Two sloping ramps led to the room, one from the street and the other from the building's private courtyard. The outer walls of the room (those furthest from the courtyard) contained regularly spaced niches, while the north-west wall of the innermost arm of the L contained an apsed niche large enough to hold a life-sized statue. The obvious interpretation for the room is as a shrine, but there are indications that it was never finished. The carefully pointed walls had never received their plaster coating, and the floor was never properly surfaced. Nevertheless the room had a long life, and was not finally filled in until *c*.360-70; it may be that an original intention to use it for religious purposes was abandoned, and instead it was used as a storeroom. The complex represented by building 1 was completed by what may have been the living quarters for the manager of the commercial premises in the north-east range. These consisted of a small square room providing an entrance into the courtyard, two corridors, one of them tessellated, and a large room, also with a tessellated floor, on the street corner at the south corner of the building. Adjacent to the main building, and no doubt associated with it, was a small subsidiary building. This had started life as a simple strip building containing a large oven and a drain; later on a smaller rear room had been added, floored with white tesserae, and probably provided living quarters for people working in the front room.

The provision in the later second century of a leat bringing water from the north of Verulamium has been commented on above. In 1995 part of a large Purbeck marble basin, approximately 1.5m in diameter, was found in the ploughsoil 30m south-east of the *macellum*; its size suggests that it was part of a public fountain, probably supplied by the Watling Street conduit. Part of a very similar Purbeck marble basin was found reused in the foundations of a third-century building in insula VIII[25] and it may not be too fanciful to imagine a series of these along the main through routes in the town. The public latrine in insula XXVIII had been flushed by water brought from the north-west in two wooden pipes. It is possible that the overflow from the fountain near the *macellum* fed these pipes.

Verulamium in the early third century seems to have enjoyed a period of unrivalled prosperity. The picture of affluent inhabitants constructing comfortable and sophisticated town houses or investing in successful commercial enterprises is reflected in the number of luxury items recorded from the town. These include bronzes of the highest quality. The statuette of Venus, found with metal awaiting reuse in an early fourth-century cellar, is well known (**colour plate 16**). Less familiar is the statuette of Mercury with his animal associates, a ram, tortoise and cock, which was found during building work in 1970 on the south side of King Harry Lane, approximately 250m outside the Silchester Gate (**colour plate 14**). Interestingly this Mercury had also been provided with a silver torc, suggesting an association with a local Celtic deity. More recently a bronze statuette of Apollo (**colour plate 15**) was found by chance on the north side of King Harry Lane, some 150m west of the spot where Mercury was found. All three bronze statuettes are of the finest quality, and the work of master craftsmen. They provide a graphic demonstration of the ability of the citizens of Verulamium to acquire the products of 'top of the range' provincial workshops.

There are many other less obvious, but no less convincing, signs of wealth. Elephant ivory was being worked by craftsmen on the Folly Lane site in the early third century; a large, uncut lump of emerald in the Verulamium Museum probably emanated from a post-Antonine jeweller's shop, while there is evidence for the working of both silver and gold in the early Antonine workshops in insula XIV. Offerings in graves in the later Roman period generally tend to be fewer than those in earlier periods. Nevertheless there are signs that at least some of the wealthier inhabitants of late second- and third-century Verulamium were concerned to carry the evidence of their worldly success into the afterlife. As in all Roman towns, the cemeteries lay outside the town boundaries, clustering along the main roads (**62**). At Verulamium the cemetery on St Stephen's Hill, 0.5km to the south of Verulamium, occupied both sides of Watling Street and originated in the mid-first century. It was still being added to for most of the third century. By now the habit of enclosing cremation burials within square or rectangular ditched enclosures had long been discontinued. Although this could be seen as a sign that family groups were breaking down, and society was becoming more mobile, many burials in the cemetery continued to cluster in fairly tight groups which may well have been delimited by hedges or light fences. Although cremation burial continued throughout the third century, inhumation became increasingly common. Many of these were now contained in coffins, usually wooden, less frequently lead-lined, and occasionally of stone (**63-4**). There is some evidence to suggest that by the third century the earlier preference for siting cemeteries on the skyline above Verulamium had been replaced by a fashion for burial near the town. Certainly most of the richer third- and early fourth-century burials lie close to main roads a short distance outside the town gates. The 'Kingsbury' burial, found in 1820 in a lead coffin (almost immediately melted down) and accompanied by exceptionally fine glass vessels, lay on the lower slope north of the river, but only about 200m outside the north-east gate. Close to the town on the south, the so-called triple tomb excavated in the 1960s in the Verulam Hills Field stood close to Watling Street some 250m outside the London Gate. Only the tile-built foundations of what had probably

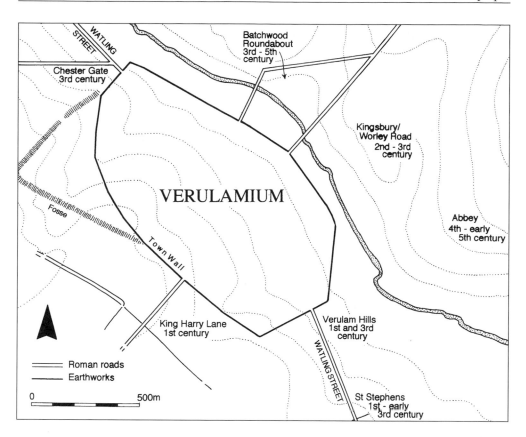

62 The Romano-British cemeteries around Verulamium. Drawn by David Williams

been an imposing monument survived. The base had been divided into three chambers or compartments, each containing a single adult inhumation, two female and one male. Nearby a child had been buried in a lead coffin and provided with an ivory staff or distaff, a silver coin of Severus Alexander, and clothing or blankets decorated with gold thread. Yet another costly monument is implied by a fragment from an elaborately carved tower tomb similar to the massive Igel tombs well known from the Rhineland, where some reached a height of over 15m. Like the German examples, the Verulamium tomb may date from the mid-second rather than the third century, but it seems to have stood in a low-lying position, close to Watling Street on the north-west of the town.[26] Not all burials were carried out with care and ceremony. A particularly bizarre discovery was uncovered during the excavation of the St Stephen's cemetery in 1986.[27] Here four adults, none of them contained in coffins, had been buried in a variety of prone, extended or crouched positions in the same pit which had been recut on the occasion of each burial from the first to late second centuries. The pit also contained remains of cremation burials. The bodies do not seem to have been deposited with any care, nor were they provided with grave offerings, although one wore iron bracelets. Whether these people had been buried in a specific place reserved for criminals, slaves or other outcasts from society is entirely a matter of

63 A late second- or third-century lead coffin, decorated on the lid and sides with a moulded pattern of scallop shells and beading. The coffin may originally have been contained within an outer, wooden coffin. Found during rescue excavations in 1989 in the St Stephen's Roman cemetery, close to Watling Street. Copyright St Albans Museum

speculation, but the presence above the last burial of a deposit of horse bones suggests the whole complex may have had a specific ritual significance.

The overall prosperity of early third-century Verulamium is underlined by the construction of two monumental arches, a new gate, and above all by the town wall. Both the monumental arches spanned Watling Street and marked the limits of the original Flavian town. Although now represented only by their flint and mortar bases, fragments of marble moulding in the area of the southern arch, close to the triangular temple, hint at ornate superstructures (**65**). At the same time a new gate, the Silchester Gate, was built on the south-west of the town. The Silchester Gate was less grandiose than either the London or the Chester Gates. It consisted of a single roadway flanked by pathways and two square towers.[28] Presumably similar gates stood at the north and 'theatre' entrances into the town, but these have never been seen (**43**).

Today it is the town wall that provides one of the most vivid reminders of St Albans' Roman antecedents (**colour plate 24**). It originally covered a total length of 3.6km and enclosed an area of just over 81ha. Above foundation level it was nearly 2.5m thick and it is estimated that it was at least 4m high, with a crenellated walkway along the top. Today all that remains above ground are a few stretches of the flint and mortar core, and not all of these lengths are accessible to the public. Below ground, however, a few courses of the original wall facing survive, directly above the massive flint and mortar footings. These tell us that the wall was once carefully faced with dressed flint with tile levelling courses at vertical intervals of approximately 1m. Built at the same time as the wall were two internal interval towers, with large semicircular bastions projecting from the opposite, outer face of the wall (**colour plate 23**). These combined towers and bastions were only provided at the south corner of the town; they serve no obvious strategic purpose and appear to have been primarily designed to provide a particularly impressive façade to anyone approaching the town from London. Behind the town wall was a clay and gravel bank. This was constructed as the wall was being built, and it was made up of material dug out of the town ditch which lay 6-7m in front of the wall (**66**). The ditch was a massive earthwork, and it too was particularly impressive south-west of the London Gate and at the south corner of the town. Although the town wall and the bank behind it extended round the whole town, it is still not certain whether the ditch ever ran along the river valley on the north-east side of Verulamium.

The best evidence for dating the construction of the town wall lies in material contained in, or sealed beneath, the bank behind the wall, but only eight sections have ever been cut through it. Inevitably therefore, dating evidence for the wall remains relatively slight. In the 1930s the Wheelers dated the town wall to the mid-second century, largely on the basis of coins and samian

64 *Reconstruction by Richard Neave (University of Manchester) of the face of the elderly man buried in the St Stephen's lead coffin. The coffin had been packed with pounded chalk, which meant that the skeleton was exceptionally well preserved, enabling the face to be reconstructed.*
Copyright St Albans Museum

ware found in and beneath the bank. Sheppard Frere challenged this dating and instead proposed a date in the later third century. He cut four sections through the town bank and found Antonine material beneath and within it. However, a section on the south-west side of insula XX produced five sherds of pottery dating to *c*.200-30 proving that the bank (and hence the wall) could not be earlier than the early third century.[29] In the past much of the argument concerning the date of the town wall has hinged on the Wheelers' discovery, in the rubble of one of the interval towers, of a hoard of coins dating from some time after 273 (the date of the latest coin in the hoard).[30] The Wheelers associated the hoard with the destruction of the tower, but Frere pointed out that it was more likely to have been deposited in the tower while it was still standing. Assuming that Frere's suggestion is correct (and it seems eminently reasonable) it only tells us that the tower was standing

65 Moulding from the third-century monumental arch across Watling Street in insula VII. Copyright St Albans Museum

sometime after 273, not when it was first built. Frere's main evidence for placing the construction of the wall in the late third century was found in a trench he dug in 1960 in insula XLII.[31] Here a thin and badly disturbed layer of gravel, which may or may not have been part of the wall bank, overlay building debris containing sherds from two flanged bowls, one of which is unlikely to be earlier than *c.*270. This debris, presumably from the Antonine building that pre-dated the town wall at this point, was not securely sealed, and Frere himself only regarded the pottery as 'potential' dating evidence for the wall. A date in the late third century for the construction of the town wall is therefore far from proven. The early third century was clearly a time when the town was enjoying a period of self-confidence and prosperity, with the disaster of the Antonine fire firmly in the past. It was a period when other towns in Roman Britain were building town walls, apparently more for reasons of prestige than for defence, and there is no reason to suppose that Verulamium lagged behind this general trend.

The construction of the town wall must have been a major and costly undertaking. It has been estimated that the wall would have required about 66,000 tons of flint; a corresponding quantity of lime mortar and tiles would also have been needed, and transport costs and labour would all have had to be organised and paid for. Several chalk and clay pits have been recorded within 1km of Verulamium, and some at least may date from this period. Much of the flint used for constructing the walls may have simply been collected from the surface of ploughed fields, but the presence of very sizeable nodules suggests that some may have been quarried, or even mined.

The third century also saw the canalisation of the Ver, an undertaking that must also have required considerable resources and expertise and which may have been linked with the construction of the town wall. A wall, built primarily to give the town prestige, should overlook something better than a stagnant marsh. At the same time the draining of the marsh may have led to a demand to a permanent boundary on this side of Verulamium. Yet another motive may have been a need to provide a sufficient head of water to drive mills further down stream. Whatever the reason, a clay and chalk bank or *levee* was constructed alongside the river, and the road linking the insula XVI temple and

66 The late 1930s' clearance of the third-century town ditch near the south corner of the town showing its original depth. Copyright St Albans Museum

theatre with the Folly Lane site raised on a pronounced *agger* which is still clearly visible today.[32]

At some point in the second or third century the principal road through Verulamium from Welwyn, and ultimately Colchester on the north to the Thames and Silchester on the south, was realigned. Up until then the through road had followed its first-century line along the north-west side of the Forum. This route forced the road to make a detour on the other side of the river in order to avoid the Folly Lane site. The route was finally 'rationalised' when the main road was resited along the south-east side of the Forum to lead to the Silchester Gate, although precisely when this happened is uncertain (*see* **34**). Some 200m south of the Folly Lane temple the new road overlay kilns dating to the first half of the second century, and on the other side of the town, outside the Silchester Gate, it overlay early second-century pottery at the point where it crossed the Wheeler ditch. Consequently the shift in the route may well have been part of the general refurbishment of the town after the Antonine fire. Alternatively, since it presumably involved the construction of a new river crossing, it may have been contemporary with the canalisation of the Ver in the third century.

Over the Roman Empire as a whole the middle and later decades of the third century were times of severe disruption and chronic inflation. While Britain as a whole seems to have escaped relatively unharmed, many of the wealthy villa owners in the countryside surrounding Verulamium appear to have suffered significant reverses in the course of the century. The Gorhambury villa suffered a period of decline in the middle of the century, and the Northchurch villa required substantial rebuilding at the end of the century, implying that the earlier villa had become dilapidated. The Park Street, Gadebridge and Lockleys villas also required extensive renovation in the early fourth century. South-west of Verulamium the villa at Boxmoor was reduced in size at the end of the third century, and one of the wing rooms in the main range was converted into a workshop. Clearly the fortunes of villa occupants varied and at present it is impossible to say how much this was due to overall economic conditions and how much to individual circumstances, such as the political allegiances of the villa owners in the turbulent political situation that persisted for so much of the century. Less is known of the fortunes of the poorer, peasant settlements where the great bulk of the population must have lived. Pottery from the enclosures and field systems above Berkhamsted that have been linked to the iron working in the upper Bulbourne valley suggests that these were abandoned in the early third century. The iron deposits seem to have been worked out, and this in itself may account for the subsequent decline seen in the nearby villas. What happened to the peasant communities themselves is still impossible to say.

In Verulamium itself the Wheelers suggested that the later third century saw the town in severe decline. Sheppard Frere qualified this by demonstrating that building continued throughout the century in insulae XX-XXII and that in these insulae at least, the later third century was a time of renewal. The situation in insulae XIV and XXVII was similar. Here plots that had lain derelict since the Antonine fire more than a century earlier were finally built over in the last quarter of the third century. A rather different picture however is emerging for other areas of the town. By the end of the century the Folly Lane site was in terminal decline while on the other side of the town, outside the Silchester Gate, suburban cellared buildings that had flourished in the early third century were now abandoned. In insula III a portico, perhaps housing stalls or shops along the street, had been erected along the north-west side of the public baths. By the end of the century however, these seem to have been semi-derelict with plaster falling off the walls and layers of humus accumulating on the floors. Without excavation it is impossible to say whether the baths themselves were in a similar state. In fact with extensive excavation still confined to only two areas of the town (the southern insulae excavated by the Wheelers and the areas around Bluehouse Hill excavated by Sheppard Frere) it is difficult to assess the overall fortunes of Verulamium, particularly in the later Roman period when relevant deposits have all too often been eroded or ploughed away. However, considerable attention has been paid to coin collections from Verulamium, particularly by Richard Reece. He has shown that after the conquest period and until the later third century, the rate of coin loss within Verulamium was within the normal range for Romano-British towns; statistically the coins lost in the town were no more or less numerous than those lost in other towns in the province. In the late third century, however, significantly more coins were dropped (and not subsequently retrieved) here than in most other Romano-British towns.[33] This pattern can be viewed in two ways. Either it is a sign that coins were almost worthless and were discarded as rubbish, or it is evidence of a thriving market, social and religious centre in a prosperous and long-established town.

5 The final centuries

The fourth-century town

> By about 273 the defences of Verulamium were in a state of tumbling decay. Houses, the theatre, were in an equally ruinous condition, and, if the considerable sample already explored is typical of the whole, Verulamium must at this time have borne some resemblance to a bombarded city. Nothing constructive belongs to this age.[1]

In 1936 the Wheelers published this description of Verulamium in the late Roman period, a description which came to encapsulate the general view of late Romano-British towns for a generation.

Over much of the area excavated by the Wheelers there was clear evidence for a surge in building activity and renovation at about the turn of the third and fourth centuries. This was described in their report as the 'Constantinian renaissance' when many of the buildings they excavated in insula I-IX were either renovated or rebuilt. They considered that it was a short-lived renaissance, however, since in their view, for much of the fourth century Verulamium was

> a Verulamium whose population had declined apparently in numbers and certainly in wealth and social standards, until it had dwindled to a sort of nucleated slum. The nucleus was the market-place and the buildings which lay around it. Beyond the nucleus stretched the old residential suburbs, now largely deserted and tumbling.[2]

R.G. Collingwood painted a still more depressing picture of the late Roman town:

> By the middle of the fourth century the . . . greater part of Verulam was uninhabited, a waste of empty land and ruined houses.[3]

As remarked in the previous chapter, and as was not infrequently the case, the conclusions reached by Sheppard Frere in his excavations between 1955 and 1961 portrayed a rather different view. For a start Frere found no evidence for a 'suspension of building activity in the third century'.[4] On the contrary, it was in about 275, at precisely the time which the Wheelers saw Verulamium as a bombarded city, that a new row of shops was built along the Watling Street frontage in insula XIV. As pointed out in the previous chapter, the number of coins lost in the town in the last quarter of the third century was above the average for Romano-British towns as a whole. Frere's excavations along Bluehouse Hill did not produce much evidence for widespread rebuilding at the beginning of the fourth century, but as many houses here had only been built in the third century there may not have been a pressing need for rebuilding only 50 years later.

Since the conclusion of Sheppard Frere's excavation campaign a considerable quantity of new evidence on the late Roman town has come to light, but even so, the total amount of reliable information remains comparatively small.

There is some suggestion of a further fire in Verulamium at the end of the third century or early in the fourth. How extensive the area affected was, or indeed whether the burnt levels recorded were not the result of several unrelated fires of similar dates, is uncertain. Burnt levels have been recorded however in the guard chambers of the Silchester Gate, in three houses in insula XIII and one in insula XIX. There was clearly extensive rebuilding in some parts of the town in the early fourth century, but we cannot yet tell whether this was because houses constructed after the Antonine fire were now simply becoming dilapidated through old age, or whether it was due to damage caused by fire.

As mentioned earlier, rather more coins were lost in Verulamium in the late third century than was normal in Romano-British towns. In the fourth century the situation was reversed, with fewer coins being lost in Verulamium compared to other towns. It is clear however that within the town and its suburbs, more coins were dropped in some places than in others. Very large numbers of later fourth-century coins were found in rubbish dumped in the theatre *cavea,* in the area around the insula XVI temple generally, from the triangular temple in insula VII and from nearby rubbish deposits in a disused cellar in insula IX.[5] Outside the town walls comparatively large numbers were also dropped a short distance south of the London gate, in Verulam Hills Field.[6] This was an area used in the third century as a cemetery, and in the late Roman period a Basilican building, just possibly a cemetery church or martyrium, stood here (below). Another concentration of late (in this case third-century) coins was recorded by Martin and Birthe Biddle in the fourth-century cemetery south of the medieval abbey of St Alban, an area where there is good reason to suggest there was a late Roman cemetery church (see below p139). By contrast the private houses, particularly those excavated by the Wheelers in the south part of the town, contained very few coins after the early fourth century. This raises the possibility that in the later fourth century coins may have been left as votive offerings on temple sites or cemetery areas (where there may have been Christian cemetery shrines). Alternatively, as their value dwindled, these coins may simply have been dumped with other rubbish outside the town or incorporated in refuse tips in the abandoned temples. At the same time there is little reason to suppose that many private houses were not still being occupied. The commercial areas of the town around the Forum could still have continued to flourish, although day-to-day transactions were increasingly paid for in kind, rather than in coin.

Figure **67** shows buildings in the town that were restored, extended or rebuilt in the last half of the fourth century. This plan is obviously far from complete, but it suggests that at least in the central area of the town, some buildings were still being constructed or renovated while others where falling into disrepair or were abandoned. This is hardly surprising. Families faced with the need to rebuild their property would be more likely to build on a nearby, but currently unbuilt-upon plot, only abandoning their existing

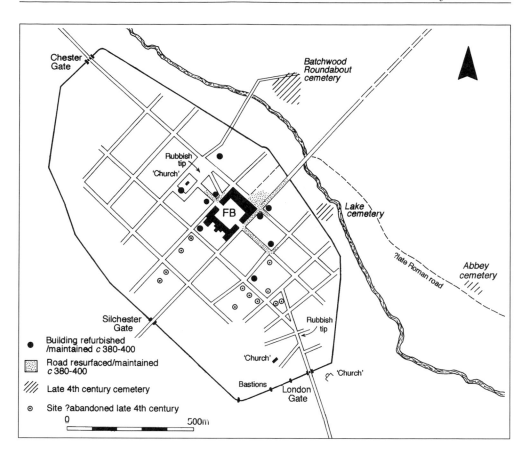

Labels in figure:
Chester Gate
Batchwood Roundabout cemetery
Rubbish tip
'Church'
FB
Lake cemetery
?late Roman road
Abbey cemetery
Silchester Gate
Rubbish tip
'Church'
'Church'
Bastions
London Gate

- Building refurbished /maintained c 380-400
- Road resurfaced/maintained c 380-400
- Late 4th century cemetery
- Site ?abandoned late 4th century

0   500m

67 Occupation in Verulamium in the last quarter of the fourth century. Drawn by David Williams

buildings when the new ones were completed. To demolish their existing house and then rebuild it on the same plot would have left them temporarily homeless. Until it is possible to excavate a complete insula and elucidate the pattern of individual plots and property boundaries, it is difficult to address questions relating to the replacement of houses or the population of the town at any one time.

It is clear however that Verulamium was never densely built up, and there must always have been open areas within its boundaries. In most Romano-British towns the latest surviving Roman levels are often overlain by a layer of black earth. Verulamium is no exception. Away from the parts of the town where there has been severe erosion, deposits of relatively stoneless, rather sandy, black soil, sometimes nearly a metre deep, have been recorded (for instance in insulae I-V and XVIII-XIX). No doubt further deposits exist elsewhere, particularly in the lower lying, less eroded parts of the town. There is considerable debate as to how the black earth deposits accumulated. The most recent study (in London) suggests they developed from the gradual weathering of dumps of domestic rubbish. At Verulamium black earth deposits were already accumulating in insula IV in the early second century, although here they were subsequently built over. In insula I black earth layers recorded by the Wheelers overlay buildings apparently abandoned in the mid-fourth century, while in insula XVIII the black earth overlay early fifth-century remains. Rubbish was clearly dumped in open spaces within the town at all phases of its history, but only in the late and post-Roman periods did sufficient quantities accumulate to form substantial deposits.

The accumulation of large quantities of domestic rubbish in the late Roman period implies continued occupation, even if the organisation of rubbish disposal was breaking down. It now looks as if in at least parts of Verulamium houses were repaired and rebuilt throughout the fourth century. In building 1, insula XXII, a cellar built some time after 350 was subsequently demolished and replaced by a substantial masonry building, presumably dating to the later decades of the fourth century.[7] Contemporary with this was a small house built in the south corner of insula XIV sometime after 375 and equipped with a mosaic floor; later still it was provided with a new hypocaust. Houses in the south corner of insula XVII, and XIII (on the north and east of the Forum), were all repaired or extended at the very end of the fourth century, while the building in the north corner of insula XII seems to have been repaired at much the same time, although the records are difficult to interpret.

This continued repair or rebuilding of private houses was reflected in public works. Streets, and the timber-lined drains and wooden water-pipes alongside them, also continued to be maintained. The stretch of Watling Street on the north-east side of the Basilica was completely resurfaced in gravel set in a fine sandy/mortar matrix, a matrix which contained a coin of the House of Valentinian (364-83). At the same time the wide gravel piazza on the south-east side of insula XIX was resurfaced in a similar manner and here the substantial make-up sealed a coin of Gratian (378-83). The stage buildings in the theatre were repaired at some time after 345, and the precinct around the insula XVI temple was substantially modified at the very end of the fourth century. The temple modifications included the provision of a new entrance on the south-east, and at the same time the original entrance on the north-east was blocked. Eleven coins of the House of Theodosius (388-95) were sealed in the construction level of the new entrance and provide the dating evidence. On the other side of Watling Street the *macellum* was evidently no longer standing in the late fourth century. Instead the site was occupied by a large building of which only the heavily robbed footings were found. All associated floor levels were absent, and little mention was made of it in the published report other than a brief reference as *late chalk foundations*.[8] The building was never completely exposed so its plan as well as its precise date are unknown, but it is clear that it was a large, possibly hall-like building constructed after the early fourth-century *macellum* had gone out of use.

While some buildings in the centre of Verulamium continued to be maintained, there is no question that some houses, particularly in the south and south-east of the town, went out of use in the second half of the fourth century. Three houses in insulae XX and XXI were either in ruins or had been deliberately demolished by the mid-fourth century, and a large house in the north corner of insula XXVIII does not appear to have been occupied after about 370.[9] Added to this is the evidence from the Wheelers' excavations where, however long the early fourth-century buildings may or may not have been in use, there was no sign of repairs and replacements in the later fourth century of the type seen in the buildings in the Forum/Theatre area. In the absence of excavation in the northern and western parts of the town, we cannot even guess the fate of houses here.

Our picture of the hinterland of Verulamium in the fourth century is also a mixed one. As in earlier periods our information comes entirely from villa sites; peasant settlements of this period within 20km of Verulamium remain unrecognised, although they must have been numerous.

At Gorhambury the villa itself seems to have been abandoned early in the fourth century, but at the same time two new barns were constructed suggesting that it was still functioning as a successful farm even if the principal residential block was no longer occupied. Nevertheless, occupation on the site ceased in the middle of the century. The Park Street villa, 4km to the south-east, was considered by its excavators to have been abandoned by the 370s. This view was based on the absence of the latest issues of Roman coins. However, two stone coffins were found on the site, one of which contained a glass flask dating from the very end of the fourth century. The evident wealth displayed by the commissioning of a 'matching pair' of stone, lead-lined coffins, suggests that the villa may have continued as a prosperous concern at least as late as the early fifth century. Other villas suggest a similarly mixed pattern. According to Graham Webster, Lockleys was burnt in *c*.340 and thereafter rebuilt and reoccupied, while nearby Dicket Mead continued to be occupied until the late fourth century. South-west of Verulamium, Northchurch villa was provided with a new bathsuite sometime after 339, but late Roman coins suggest that the nearby Boxmoor villa was abandoned in the mid-fourth century. At Gadebridge the villa was restored in the early fourth century and 20 or 30 years later was provided with an enlarged, open air swimming pool. By the middle of the century however the baths had fallen out of use, and shortly afterwards the main residential building was demolished, although a cottage, perhaps housing a bailiff or tenant, continued to be occupied, and coins have been found on the site down to the early fifth century. Pottery and other finds from Mackerye End in the Lea valley also suggest continued occupation on the site of this presumed villa at the very end of the Roman period.

The fifth century and beyond

In the past, views of the final years of Roman Verulamium have verged on the sensational and catastrophic. Grover writing about the town in 1869 described it as follows:

> In the fifth century the Roman soldier goes away; the barbarians rush from their mountains in the north, the Irish pirates follow in their wake, ruin and desolation mark their track. The Saxon comes and seals the final doom of civilisation — by wholesale disendowment and disestablishment. Behold Verulam on fire, its roofs fall — all is destroyed save the blackened walls. It must have presented a gloomy and ruinous scene for many hundred years.[10]

This extract summarises a view of the post-Roman period that was still widely held up until comparatively recent times. Even in 1936, the Wheelers, relying on evidence from their excavations here in the early 1930s, concluded that:

> The rough clay-patching of the floors of the Roman houses represents the
> ultimate occupation of them and denotes a return to a condition of barbarism
> far more complete and negative than that from which Verulamium had
> originally sprung . . .[11]

It was another 25 years before any real doubt was thrown on this rather depressing view
of the final fate of Roman Verulamium. Sheppard Frere's excavations between 1955 and
1961 were the first to provide a significant new insight into the state of Verulamium in the
decades leading up to the final withdrawal of the remnants of the Roman field army from
Britain in 409, and the half-century thereafter.

Between 1957 and 1959 Frere excavated two late Roman buildings just outside the
north-west entrance into the Forum, between it and the theatre. The smaller of these
buildings was a four-roomed house, resting on flint and mortar foundations in the south
corner of insula XIV. One room contained both a mosaic and a hypocaust, and on the north
side of the building was a connecting corridor or verandah, which had also been provided
with a tessellated floor. Sealed in the foundation of the hypocaust was a coin of Valentinian
I, dating from between 367 and 375, showing that the house cannot have been constructed
before the last quarter of the fourth century at the earliest. It was then used for a
considerable period. A bread oven, in what was presumably the kitchen, was completely
rebuilt, at least one floor was renewed, and the tessellated floor in the verandah had become
so worn that it had to be extensively patched. Later still the house was completely
remodelled to form a rectangular, two-roomed house with a projecting wing at the north-
east end. This phase can hardly be earlier than the early fifth century, but it contained both
a mosaic floor and a hypocaust.[12] The larger of the two late Roman houses excavated by
Frere had undergone a similarly protracted sequence of construction. It stood in the east
corner of insula XXVII and had 18 rooms on the ground floor alone; there was also some
evidence for an upper storey. Sheppard Frere originally dated the house to the late fourth
century.[13] This dating is now being questioned, but it seems certain that the building was
still being maintained at the very end of the fourth century. Later still the house was entirely
demolished and replaced by a large hall-like building, measuring at least 34m x 14m. This
had been well built with substantial flint and mortar footings, supported by small
buttresses. Where the foundations overlay earlier pits, they had been further supported by
timber piles (**68**). These very solid foundations had subsequently been cut through by a
carefully dug trench accommodating a timber water pipe bringing water from the south
(presumably supplied by a spring further up the slope) to an area somewhere north of the
buttressed building but beyond the limits of the excavated area. Both the buttressed
building and the water pipe must date from a period well within the fifth century.

The importance of the excavation of both these building sequences was that for the
first time construction and occupation of masonry based houses could be conclusively
demonstrated as persisting well into the fifth century. Previously, occupation in the centre
of Verulamium had been seen as having already declined to the point of squalor by the end
of the fourth century. Collingwood described the area between the Forum and Theatre as

68 Posts underpinning the mid-fifth-century buttressed building in insula XXVII. Reproduced courtesy of the St Albans Museum Service, copyright reserved

an area where 'a shrunken and impoverished population lived in slum conditions'. In the years since the publication of Frere's excavations a considerable amount of new evidence concerning the final years of Roman Verulamium has come to light. Unfortunately there are particular difficulties involved in the study of the late and post-Roman town.

Probably the most serious handicap with which anyone looking at late Roman Verulamium has to contend is the damage caused by erosion and ploughing. Late and post-Roman deposits are clearly particularly vulnerable to this sort of damage. These are the deposits that are shallowest in terms of buried depth, and at Verulamium they have not been protected by overlying medieval deposits. It has recently become clear just how extensive the damage caused by ploughing has been. In the past it has sometimes been argued that ploughing would not have destroyed flint and mortar footings or *opus signinum* floors. Test pits dug across the whole of the northern half of Verulamium in 2000 demonstrated, however, that over significant parts of this area the latest surviving Roman surfaces were directly overlain by a mere 20cm of ploughsoil. Furthermore, plough furrows were clearly visible cutting through both masonry footings and the mortar floors confirming the view that these remains are no match for modern agricultural machinery.

The tendency for late Roman buildings in Verulamium to be provided with chalk footings, combined with the persistence of traditional methods of building the superstructures in clay and timber, means that these late buildings are, if anything, less resistant to damage than the flint and mortar foundations commoner in the later second and third centuries. The sloping nature of the land over so much of the Roman town and the resulting natural erosion has no doubt compounded the damage. Already in the late 1950s Sheppard Frere noted that 'extreme denudation by the plough' had destroyed evidence for the latest occupation in insulae XX and XXI; modern agricultural machinery is generally heavier than that used in the 1940s and it is more than likely that by now late Roman levels have been removed over substantial areas of the town. It has to be constantly borne in mind that the surviving remains probably only represent a fraction of the original late Roman town.

Patches of clay or gravel, surviving in the hollows caused by subsidence in third- and fourth-century floors, are not uncommon in the houses of later Roman Verulamium. These patches must be all that survives of still later surfaces (**69**). It is unfortunate that the major advances in excavation techniques that enabled substantial post-Roman timber halls and other buildings to be recognised in fifth-century Wroxeter came too late to be applied in the large scale excavations in and around Verulamium in the 1950s and '60s.[14] These techniques require meticulous excavation and recording over substantial areas, the sort of areas which have not become available for excavation within Verulamium since the early 1960s. Small trenches excavated in the town in the 1980s (below p141) suggest that ephemeral remains of structures of similar date almost certainly survive in Verulamium but it is impossible to determine their true character and extent in the restricted excavation trenches that are typical of modern work here. In summary, the dearth of evidence for occupation at this period may, at least in part, be due to the absence of excavation over wider areas, rather than an absence of surviving remains.

Even in areas where later Roman deposits have been recognised, it is usually extremely difficult to date them accurately. As in Roman Britain generally, the use of pottery in Verulamium gradually declined. The earlier fourth-century flood of coarse pottery into the town from kilns in the Hadham, Oxford, and later on in the New Forest area had been reduced to a trickle by the end of the century. After the early fifth century, apart from the occasional handmade jar apparently made locally, people in Verulamium seem to have relied on metal or wood vessels, supplemented perhaps by fine ceramic table ware kept as heirlooms and brought out for special occasions.

In 407 the final remnants of the Roman field army were withdrawn from Britain, and the supply of new coinage, which up until then had come into the province as pay for the army, also dried up. In the absence of both pottery and coins, the principal tools for dating the final years of Roman Verulamium are largely lacking. Added to this, material from apparently unstratified levels overlying late Roman buildings has not always been retained by excavators in the past. Even where late deposits survive and are recognised, the date at which buildings were finally abandoned can be very difficult to estimate. Houses were presumably kept free of rubbish, and if, as appears to have been the case, rubbish was dumped well away from buildings, it may be difficult to date their final use with any degree of confidence.

In spite of all these difficulties it is beginning to be possible to provide a broad-brush picture of life in Verulamium in the post Roman period. Certainly the picture of early fifth-century Verulamium painted by the Wheelers and Collingwood needs to be substantially modified.

It is now clear that at the end of the fourth century Verulamium was still equipped with most amenities of a major provincial Roman town. The only exception may have been the public baths in insula III. Even this is not certain, however. Although the north-eastern portico was derelict by the end of the third century, this need not necessarily have been the case with the Baths themselves. Elsewhere the water supply and defences were all maintained, while at least one of the town's temples, the *macellum* and the Forum/Basilica complex were all apparently in regular use. The streets, at any rate in the core of the town, were also still being conscientiously maintained. Coins contained in the make-up for the final resurfacing of Watling Street, north of the Basilica date from the final decades of the fourth century. At the same time the

69 *A late Roman crossbow brooch from the courtyard building in insula III. Overall length 8.1cm.* Copyright St Albans Museum

wide gravelled piazza that had existed since the late first century outside the north-east entrance into the Basilica was carefully resurfaced. The roadside drains alongside the streets surrounding the Basilica continued to be cleaned out while the early fifth-century water pipe in insula XXVII is evidence for a continued water supply to at least part of the town.

The theatre had gone out of use by the late fourth century but this may have been more to do with the decline of the pagan cult with which it was undoubtedly associated, than a decline in urban life. Certainly the amount of rubbish that then accumulated in the disused *cavea* implies not only a substantial population nearby but also a communal system for disposing of refuse.

In the past a particular style of bronze buckles, and strap ends, with a distinctive type of decoration based ultimately on zoomorphic designs, has been seen as part of the uniform worn by Germanic mercenaries serving in the late Roman army. Their occurrence in late Roman towns was in turn taken as suggesting the presence of detachments of late Roman mercenaries, stationed here as added protection. More recent work suggests that this type of metalwork was produced in late Roman factories in

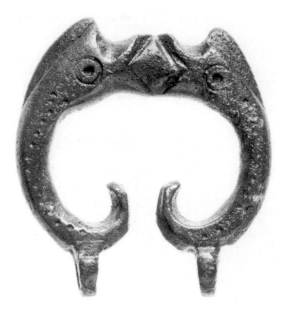

northern Gaul, and was used both by the late Roman army (which by this time contained a large proportion of 'Germanic' units and mercenaries) and by officials in the civil service. Verulamium has produced two small bronze fittings decorated in this style; both were in later deposits, and both came from the general area of the theatre. Their presence near the centre of the town where they were probably accidentally lost, need reflect nothing more than the presence here of late Roman tax assessors (**70**).

70 *A zoomorphic buckle decorated with stylised dolphins, found near the Theatre.* Copyright St Albans Museum

Alban and evidence for Christianity

Since the time of Constantine in the early fourth century, Christianity had been the state religion, and although it was not universally adopted, it would be reasonable to expect some indication of it in Verulamium by the end of the Roman period. Bede, writing in the mid-eighth century, explicitly mentions a Romano-British church still standing at Verulamium, and one that was sufficiently well known to attract visitors in his own day. It is consequently somewhat surprising to note that small, portable items with Christian symbols are as yet completely absent from the town. On the other hand three late Roman buildings have been interpreted as Christian churches in the past (**71**).

For many years the blocked north-eastern entrance in the precinct around the insula XVI temple has been seen as a possible indication of the conversion of the temple to a church at the very end of the fourth century. Unfortunately, apart from this blocking, there is no firm evidence for the temple's dedication, either in the earlier Roman period, or in its final phase in the early fifth century, so a change of use in the late Roman period is by no means certain. The only excavations that have taken place on the site were those of A.W.G. Lowther in 1934,[15] and these do not appear to have been very extensive. Until further work is possible on the site, therefore, the question of Christian use of the insula XVI temple must remain unproven.

The second building to be identified as a possible church was recorded during tree planting in insula IX in 1937.[16] The walls had been entirely robbed out, and no stratified levels survived. It was interpreted as a church solely on the basis of its plan: a rectangle 12.5m wide and 15.8m long, with square projection at both ends. The footings for the north-eastern projection, however, were much heavier and deeper than those of the rest

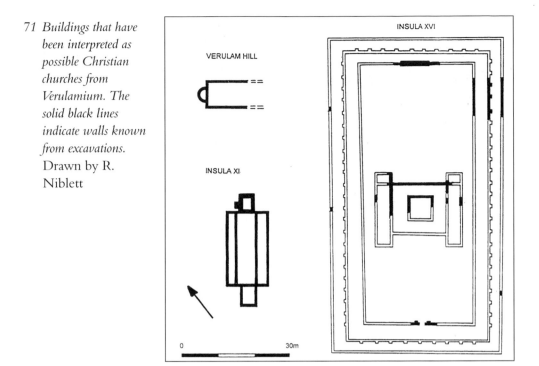

71 Buildings that have been interpreted as possible Christian churches from Verulamium. The solid black lines indicate walls known from excavations. Drawn by R. Niblett

of the building, and the question arises whether it was in fact a small tower like granary, attached perhaps to a barn. A rather similar arrangement is known as part of a larger, late Roman building in insula II.

The third possible church lies just outside the town on the Verulam Hills Field site.[17] Here the eroded foundations of a flint and mortar building were excavated in 1966. Only part of the plan was recovered, but it had clearly been a rectangular structure, 3.6m wide and at least 6m long, with a semicircular apse at its north-west end; its initial date was uncertain as all stratified layers had been eroded away. The identification as a church again rests largely on the basis of the plan, although it has also been suggested that its position, approximately 50m to the north-west of small third-century inhumation cemetery, could indicate its origin as a cemetery church, on the grave of a leading early Christian. None of the Roman burials show any specifically Christian characteristics however, while a fragment of a bronze life-size statue decorated with a winged cupid, found in ploughsoil over the building and almost certainly derived from it, does not suggest a Christian function for it. Added to this, it is worth noting that the building stood near the corner of a first-century ditched enclosure which contained mid-first-century burials and an apparently ritual pit (above p45, 58). Taken together the evidence for a Christian use for the Verulam Hills Field building is far from conclusive.

The main evidence for a Christian community in late Roman Verulamium comes not from archaeological evidence but from references in documentary sources to the late Roman martyr Alban. Alban apparently lived in Verulamium and was martyred sometime in the later Roman period; traditionally he is the earliest British martyr. The actual date of his martyrdom however is a matter of dispute. The evidence for Alban comes from four early sources; from a *Passio Albani* (an account of the martyrdom of Alban), from references in *Vita sancti Germani* (a life of St Germanus) by Constantius of Lyons (writing in the late fifth century), from a diatribe by the sixth-century monk Gildas, and from Bede's *Historia Ecclesiastica Gentis Anglorum*, written in the early eighth century. The *Passio Albani* survives in three versions, one of which describes Alban's martyrdom as taking place under a *severus imperator* which is variously translated as the emperor Severus (AD 192-211) or 'the harsh emperor'. Some scholars have argued that the whole passage allows the trial and execution of Alban to be dated to 211 when Severus was in Britain, with both his sons, Caracalla and Geta. While Caracalla was campaigning with his father in Scotland, the administrative and judicial affairs would have been left to the younger son Geta, who at that time had the title of Caesar. Not all scholars accept this argument, and at present there is no consensus as to the date of Alban's martyrdom, other than it must have occurred sometime in the third or fourth centuries.

Another early reference to Alban comes in Constantius' *vita sancti Germani* which he wrote in Gaul at the end of the fifth century. Constantius described the visit by St Germanus, bishop of Auxerre, to Britain in 429. The purpose of the visit was to suppress the Pelagian heresy which had attracted many supporters in Britain. After successfully confronting the British bishops in some unnamed town (possibly London), Germanus proceeded to visit the site of St Alban's martyrdom and burial. Unfortunately Constantius does not actually name the place itself, although it is clear from the account that both the place of martyrdom and the martyr's grave were known, and that there was a martyrium of some sort at least on the site of the grave. Furthermore, he tells us that:

> Germanus tore up a lump of earth from the actual spot where the martyr's blood had flowed. This desecration was justified, since the stain of the blood could still be seen. This was a great sign shown clearly to all men, of how the martyr's blood had reddened the earth as his persecutor grew pale[18]

It is not difficult to see this description of the soil on the site of the martyrdom as an allusion to the local clay with flints subsoil, which, distinctly orange in its upper, oxidized levels, occurs locally within a few centimetres of the surface over many areas on the upper slopes.

Like Constantius, the author of the *Passio* also failed to say specifically that the martyrdom took place at Verulamium, although here again the account of the martyrdom includes details that could easily apply to the town.

> . . . He was led like a lamb to the slaughter to a place where a fast flowing river ran between the city wall and the arena where he was to be executed . . . as he passed to the far bank he saw a considerable crowd of people, both men and women, of all ranks and ages, no doubt drawn there by Divine purpose, to follow the saint to his martyrdom; so many that it was hardly possible for them to cross the bridge that evening . . . Meanwhile the holy martyr with the crowd, climbed a hill which rose up in a very pleasant and suitable way about five hundred paces from the river bank [or arena]. It was decorated and decked out

with different kinds of flowers. It was not a cliff or steep slope but stretched down gradually, evenly and with a natural setting . . .[19]

The earliest source that mentions Verulamium in connection with Alban is the British monk Gildas, who was writing in Britain probably in about the middle of the sixth century. Gildas tells us that Alban was a citizen of Verulamium, but does not actually say he was martyred here. It is not until Bede, writing in the early eighth century, that we get the explicit statement that Alban was executed and buried at Verulamium.

There is however growing evidence that a later Roman cemetery church may have been established on or near the site on which the medieval abbey of St Alban was ultimately established (**colour plate 24**). This lies the required 500 paces outside the Roman town, on the other side of the river, and on the brow of the hill. This was a site which two German scholars, Wilhelm Meyer and Wilhelm Levison, suggested as that of an early cemetery church or martyrium, later replaced by the Saxon monastery.[20] It was to test this hypothesis that Martin and Birthe Biddle undertook a programme of excavation and research on the south side of the Abbey between 1983 and 1995. As a result of this work we now have a much clearer understanding of what was going on close to the site of the medieval abbey in the late and immediately post-Roman period.[21]

As far as the late and post-Roman history of Verulamium is concerned, the most important result of the Biddles' excavation was the discovery of an early fourth-century cemetery on the hill where the Abbey stood later. This cemetery was still in use at the end of the fourth century, although the excavators noted that 'It is unlikely that the graves are later than the fifth century at the latest'. Twenty graves were excavated in 1982-4 and 1994-5, all on the south side of the medieval abbey. They were aligned east/west and were contained in wooden coffins, but the absence of grave goods made them difficult to date. Their density and distribution suggested that they lay on the edge of a larger cemetery, the core of which lay further south, and this may have been the area in which a late Roman cemetery church was sited. The recent excavations demonstrated, however, that in the late Roman period a gravel surface had been laid on which numerous late Roman coins were dropped. This suggests that by the later third and fourth centuries substantial numbers of people were already coming to this particular cemetery. The same general area has produced an early fifth-century penannular brooch, a fifth- or sixth-century disc attachment, and a sixth-century silver hand pin; all these scattered items hint at continued use of the hill in the later fifth and sixth centuries. However, whether they were dropped accidentally, or deliberately deposited at a martyr's shrine or in a cemetery church, is a question that only further excavation will resolve.

The area south of the Abbey, however, is not the only cemetery with very late Roman graves. Fifty-three inhumation burials have been found on the north bank of the river 250m outside the North Gate of the Roman town. Here again it was extremely difficult to date the cemetery although several graves had been cut through layers of rubble overlying a Roman cellar demolished sometime in the second half of the fourth century. The absence of grave-goods and the alignment of the graves suggested that the burials were Christian, while their stratigraphical position indicated a very late Roman or post-Roman date (**72**). The 'pock-marks' occasionally seen from the air in the field west of the

72 An early fifth-century burial from Batchwood roundabout. Copyright St Albans Museum

roundabout suggest that the cemetery may have been extensive, stretching a further 150m in that direction.

Together these burials make a total of 73 graves dating from the last decades of Roman rule, if not later. Compared to the enormous fourth- and early fifth-century cemetery at Poundbury, outside Dorchester, which contained nearly 4000 graves, the numbers from Verulamium are very modest. We can be sure, however, that these represent only a fraction of the total, and cannot be taken as any indication as to the size of population in late Roman Verulamium.

Verulamium in the sixth and seventh centuries

Extending the maintenance of Romano-British occupation within Verulamium until the mid- or even late fifth century does not, however, really address the main problem of what happened here between the later fifth century and the early eighth. In particular it does not answer two basic questions: to what extent did a Romano-British way of life survive, and could this way of life be considered in any way as urban? The evidence for continued building well into the fifth century outside the north-west gate of the Forum, in insulae XIV and XXVII, could simply represent a single elite family maintaining their estate, while the surrounding area steadily declined into a mere scattering of peasant hovels, in which the drastically reduced and impoverished remnants of the former population scratched a living amid the crumbling ruins. In other words, should we see the emergence of the depressing slum which Collingwood and others saw as existing in the late fourth century as simply being deferred to the late fifth?

By the end of the fourth century, occupation within Verulamium was beginning to concentrate in the central area of the town, around the Forum/Basilica (**67**). This is a trend that continued through the fifth century (**75**). There are now a growing number of sites in and around the town where there is evidence for timber buildings which may well date from this period. Indeed it is remarkable that on nearly every excavation carried out in Verulamium since the late 1970s, some evidence for post-Roman timber structures has been recovered. On the other hand, the type of deposits found suggest very different buildings to those excavated by Frere in insulae XIV and XXVII.

Typical of these deposits are those found in insulae XVIII. In the west corner of this insula, remains of what must be post-Roman occupation have been recorded over the latest levels in a substantial late Roman house, complete with flint and mortar foundations and tessellated and mosaic floors. This house seems to have been occupied as late as the early fifth century.[22] At some time after it had finally gone out of use, however, a timber building was erected over the earlier floors and provided with a small oven and an open hearth. Very similar remains have been found in the adjacent insula XIII, on the east side of the Forum. In 1955, remains of a post-Roman wattle and daub 'screen' around a small hearth were found overlying the remains of a fourth-century building approximately 30m to the south-west of the insula XVIII house (**73**). In the south corner of the same insula, excavations between 1986 and 1988 uncovered an open yard, first laid out in the third century. Sometime at the very end of the fourth or early in the fifth century it was resurfaced and provided with four or five tile-built ovens, showing at least two periods of use. Finally a new surface was laid over the whole area on which (ultimately) two middens accumulated. By this time the use of pottery had practically died out; although contained in one midden, together with fragments of heavily weathered pottery derived from earlier periods, was part of a small, handmade mug in coarse local fabric.

Remains of what may be still later occupation were found in 1986 when beam slots and postholes capable of accommodating substantial timbers were excavated in a small trench on the edge of Watling Street to the south of insula II (**74**). Here again, nothing was found that could be used to date the remains and all that can be said is that they were constructed after the final use of the Roman building, and at a time when pottery and coins were no longer used. Similarly the open piazza in front of the north-east entrance to the Basilica that had been carefully maintained as an open space since the late first century, and had been resurfaced at the very end of the fourth, was finally built over. At some stage in the post Roman period a sub-rectangular timber structure resting on cill beams and measuring 5m by at least 3m was terraced into the latest Roman surface. Here again it was difficult to date as it belonged to a period when pottery was not in general use, but it pre-dated a twelfth- to fourteenth-century extension to St Michael's graveyard.

Not only does the absence of associated material make it almost impossible to date this late or post-Roman occupation, but because excavation has been confined to very small areas, it has not even been possible to recover meaningful plans. Rather more complete plans of four small buildings, however, have been excavated a short distance north of the town, on the Folly Lane/Oysterfield site. After the end of the Roman period the road from Verulamium to Welwyn and Braughing degenerated into a shallow hollow-way, following a braided, rather sinuous route up the slope. Three of the buildings used an earlier road surface to provide a solid base for their floors, and all fronted onto the hollow-way. The buildings were rectangular and were supported by sturdy wooden uprights set in postholes packed with broken Roman querns and building material. In only one case was the complete plan recovered, but this suggested a building measuring 7 x 3m with a possible additional extension at one end (**colour plate 25**).[23] A very similar building stood to the south of Verulamium, on the site of the Roman cemetery on St Stephen's Hill.[24] No floor levels survived in any of these buildings themselves and their precise date is uncertain. In areas immediately adjacent to the buildings on the Folly Lane/Oysterfield

73 *An early post-Roman*
tiled hearth (right
hand side with
horizontal scale)
excavated in 1955 in
the Verulamium
museum car park in
insula XIII.
Copyright St
Albans Museum

site, however, the layers of mud that had built up in the hollow-way contained numerous sherds of handmade, chaff-tempered pottery, and the obvious inference is that the pottery derives from the houses. This type of coarse, rather featureless pottery is generally dated to between the fifth and eighth centuries, although in some areas, including areas around Aylesbury and Dunstable (and possibly Verulamium), it may not have appeared much before the seventh century. It has also been found in the area south of the Abbey, and in a small inhumation cemetery south-east of King Harry Lane on the south side of Verulamium. This cemetery is dated by grave goods to the late seventh and early eighth century. It lay 200m outside the Silchester Gate of the Roman town, and apparently represents a small group of Germanic settlers established here in the middle Saxon period. Two of the burials contained vessels in chaff-tempered fabric, but this does not mean to say that this sort of pottery is a characteristic of Germanic settlement in the area; it may simply be the pottery that was in use by both indigenous and immigrant populations in the post-Roman period.

Figure **75** shows the sites for which there is some evidence for use, if not occupation sometime between *c*.450 and 700. It suggests that while there were still people living in what had been the centre of the Roman town, there was also a straggle of occupation along the main roads leading out of it to the south-west and north-east. Comparison between figures **67** and **75** suggests that the pattern of post-Roman occupation was simply a development of a trend that started in the late fourth century. Furthermore, comparison with figures **19**, **31** and **35**, showing occupation in Verulamium at the end of the Iron Age and in the conquest period, suggests that in the post-Roman period the settlement pattern reverted to one very similar to that which had existed 400 years earlier. The major

74 Early post-
   Roman slots
   and postholes
   cutting through
   the edge of
   Watling Street
   in insula II.
   Copyright St
   Albans
   Museum

difference between the two patterns relates to the scattered finds south of the medieval abbey, but whether these reflect occupation here, or were offerings or casual losses at a martyrium, has not yet been resolved.

Reuse of Roman buildings

Interspersed with the post-Roman timber buildings there were almost certainly some surviving late Roman buildings. Bede's reference to a Roman church of 'wondrous workmanship' that was still being visited in his own day implies the continued use of at least one late Roman building, albeit a very special one. We do not know when the major public buildings of the town were demolished. There is no evidence for the violent destruction of late Roman buildings, but the wholesale demolition of a building the size of the Forum/Basilica would itself have demanded considerable organisation and manpower. At Wroxeter, the Basilica attached to the town baths continued to be used for most of the fifth century, although at the end of the century the portico was used for market stalls, and a number of small timber or wattle and daub structures were put up in the interior. It was gradually demolished piecemeal in the later fifth and early sixth centuries. In about the middle of the sixth century the surviving remains were finally dismantled, and replaced by over 30 timber buildings; although some of these had originally been substantial structures, the surviving traces of them were extremely ephemeral.[25] Whether a comparable sequence occurred at Verulamium, or whether the Forum/Basilica complex at Verulamium was still standing largely intact, in the fifth to eighth centuries, are questions to which there is, as yet, no answer. The internal walls of the Basilica must have been demolished by the tenth century when St Michael's church was built in what would have been the interior, but it is conceivable that the buildings on the south side of the Forum were still standing. Excavations immediately north-east of the

143

Basilica, on the site of an extension to the Verulamium Museum, revealed a late, partly mortared wall, post-dating the latest phase of the Basilica portico and running north from it. Surrounding deposits of black earth had been much disturbed when the area formed part of a farmyard in the post-medieval period and it is difficult to say whether the wall represents use of the site in the post or sub-Roman period, or whether it was associated with a medieval or later farm.[26]

It appears from a reference in the Abbey chronicles that in the tenth century there were still people living in the Roman town. Even in the twelfth century, during the reign of Stephen, the *Gesta Abbatum* refers to people living in what it referred to as a *propugnaculum*. This building is described as being on the east side of Kingsbury (the 'King's burh') but separate from it.[27] The identity of Kingsbury itself poses something of a problem. It is first referred to in the tenth century although without any description of its precise location. Throughout the medieval period and until the eighteenth century Kingsbury was the name used to describe the area between St Michael's church, on the site of the Roman Basilica, and the river crossing. In the nineteenth century, however, theories based on the belief that this part of Verulamium lay under a massive lake (see above p15 and figure **3**) in the Roman and subsequent period led to the identification of the higher ground, on the north side of Fishpool street (on the other side of the river to the Roman town) as the site of Kingsbury (**75** and **colour plate 1**). Research has so far failed to produce firm evidence that occupation was focused here in the early or middle Saxon period.[28] Excavation has also failed to find any sign of a defence on the northern or western sides, and although a substantial ditch is known on the east and south side (where it was recut in the sixteenth or seventeenth century) its initial date is unknown; it may well have been a medieval or early post-medieval boundary. The only evidence for early, post-Roman occupation in this area is provided by postholes from two timber buildings. These are undated but appear to be a similar type to the post-Roman buildings on the Folly Lane/Oysterfield and King Harry Lane sites. On the other hand, there clearly was a ditch (albeit as yet undated) on the north side of Fishpool Street. It is just possible that there were two burhs in late Saxon St Albans, just as there were two burhs at Hertford and Bedford.[29]

It is quite possible that the medieval references to Kingsbury in fact refer to an area within the Roman town, quite possibly in the Forum/Basilica area. In this case the *propugnaculum* could refer to one of the gateways into the Roman town, probably the London Gate. It is quite feasible that this was occupied in the post-Roman period, just as the buildings in Wroxeter, referred to above, were apparently still in use in the fifth and early sixth centuries.

So what is the current picture of Verulamium between the early fifth and late seventh centuries? Certainly it is a very different one to that of the late fourth-century town. The evidence of the sort found by Sheppard Frere for early fifth-century building in what was still a Roman manner has not been found elsewhere in very late, or post-Roman Verulamium. Many houses certainly were abandoned, either, as the Wheelers thought, in the mid-fourth century, or as now seems more likely, during the early years of the fifth. Although at least some buildings appear to have been replaced in the fifth century, most new buildings were now in timber and were much smaller and simpler in plan than their predecessors. There are two points that should be borne in mind however. Firstly this was

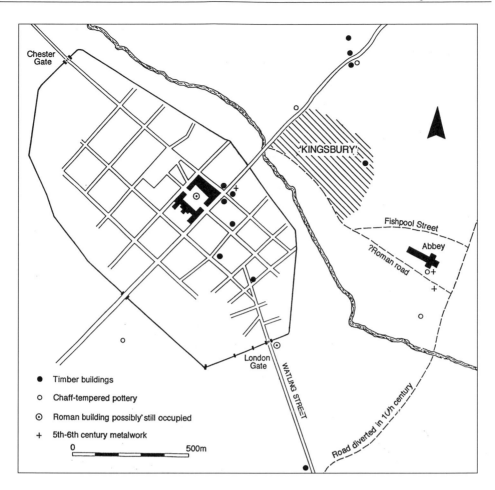

75 Occupation in early post-Roman Verulamium. Drawn by David Williams

a gradual process; some buildings, like those in insulae XX and XXI, had fallen out of use by the last quarter of the fourth century, while others clearly continued to be maintained well into the fifth century. Secondly there is no reason to think that the fifth- and sixth-century timber buildings were ramshackle hovels; there were probably reasonably substantial and weatherproof houses, albeit of relatively modest dimensions and basic plan.

The population of post-Roman Verulamium may well have declined, but this is difficult to estimate in the absence of any reliable figure for the town's population in its heyday. Yet another difficulty is that the evidence for the houses of the bulk of the Romano-British population is extremely sparse. As has been stressed above, we know little about the houses of either the rural or the urban poor. It is possible that at least some of the apparently empty areas which are so marked a feature of Roman Verulamium were occupied by timber buildings, resting on cill beams and with beaten earth floors. These would not show up on air photos or geophysics, and might have been missed in the narrow trial trenches cut particularly in the 1930s and earlier. The simple timber buildings, like those fronting the hollow-way on the Folly Lane/Oysterfield site, may not have been so very different to buildings occupied by the urban and rural poor in the Roman period.

Unfortunately even less is known about the immediate hinterland of Verulamium in the sixth and seventh centuries than is known about the post-Roman town itself. Although many of the villas south and west of Verulamium seem to have gone out of use in the course of the fourth century this is not to say that the land was no longer farmed, or that there was extensive rural depopulation. Villa owners may simply have moved away, leaving the land to be farmed by tenants. Sadly in the Verulamium area our knowledge of the local environment at the time remains almost entirely conjectural. At this period this is hardly surprising; the absence of excavated deposits almost inevitably means a corresponding absence of environmental data. Even where fifth-century or later remains have been excavated, the deposits have lain too close to the modern surface to allow for uncontaminated soil samples to be retrieved. This lack is one that future excavations may be able to rectify; potentially environmental evidence could reflect significant settlement and population changes in the post-Roman and early Saxon periods. At the time of writing, however, it looks as if early Saxon infiltration in the area was limited. Until the appearance of the small Saxon cemetery off King Harry Lane in the eighth century,[30] there are no known early Saxon cemeteries nearer than Luton, 20km to the north on the Icknield Way. There seems to be a general dearth not only of early Saxon cemeteries, but also of early Saxon pottery and brooches, and early Saxon place names within about 20km of Verulamium.

The Anglo-Saxon Chronicle contains a reference to a battle at Biedcanford in 571, a battle in which the British were defeated by the south Saxons. Biedcanford has been identified as Bedford, and it is suggested that as a result the Vale of Aylesbury came under Saxon control. Not all scholars agree with the identification of Biedcanford as Bedford however, and even if the two were the same, the British defeat need not necessarily have resulted in Anglo-Saxon domination of areas east and north of the Chiltern scarp. In the 1930s Wheeler suggested that area around Verulamium in the south-west Chilterns formed a 'sub-Roman enclave' with little or no early Saxon penetration. An independent British 'enclave' around Verulamium could have survived for another century after the battle of Biedcanford, wherever this took place. The Tribal Hidage, a tribal list dating from the later seventh or eighth centuries, mentions the *Cilternsaete* (the inhabitants of the Chilterns). These people are sometimes assumed to have been the remnants of the Romano-British population, but there is no proof that this was the case. In the early eighth century Bede's comments indicate a settled community at St Albans, and although he does not identify this as being either Saxon or British. Bede also tells us that Verulamium was now commonly called Waeclingacaestir, a statement that is supported by a Saxon charter which refers to the *Waeclingas* (the followers of Waecla).[31] This place name suggests that Waecla's followers were probably Anglo-Saxons, but Bede's insistence that the late Roman church commemorating St Alban, and the traditions associated with it, were still being respected implies that the population also included a significant British element. Seventy years after Bede, St Albans enters history when Offa established the monastery of St Alban close to the site of the existing cathedral. As discussed in the first chapter of this book, it was the needs of this abbey that accounted for the final destruction of Verulamium.

Notes

Chapter 1

1 Translation Niblett, R.H. from an entry in the *Gesta Abbatum Monasterii Sancti Albani, Vol 1,* 20, Riley H.T. (ed.), 1867, Rolls Society.
2 *Gesta, ibid.,* Translation Niblett, R.H.
3 Shrimpton J., *The Antiquities of Verulam and St Albans,* Ritchie C.I.A. (ed.), 1966, St Albans and Hertfordshire Architectural and Archaeological Society.
4 Stukeley, W., 1721, *Vestigia Romanorum.*
5 Gough, Richard, 1780, *British Topography: Hertfordshire* (for the cemetery). Also *Archaeologia* vol.17, 1814, 335-6 (for the Kingsbury burial).
6 Brayley, E.W., 1808, *Beauties of England and Wales Vol.VII.* 92-3; Anon., 1815, *History of Verulam and St Albans,* G. Shaw (publisher).
7 Grover, J.W., 1869, 'Verulam and Pompeii compared', *Journal of the British Archaeological Association, 26,* 45-52.
8 Wheeler, R.E.M. and T.V., 1936, *Verulamium, a Belgic and Two Roman Cities,* Research Report of the Society of Antiquaries of London no. XI.
9 Collingwood, R.G. and Myres, J.N.L., 1936, *Roman Britain and the English Settlements;* Richmond, Ian, 1947, *Roman Britain.*
10 Frere, S.S., 1964, 'Verulamium: three Roman Cities', *Antiquity 38,* 103-12; 1972, *Verulamium Excavations: Volume I,* Research Report of the Society of Antiquaries of London no. XXVIII; 1983, *Verulamium Excavations: Volume II,* Research Report of the Society of Antiquaries of London no. XLI Oxford; 1984, *Verulamium Excavations: Volume III,* Oxford University Committee for Archaeology Monograph 1.
11 For a discussion of the reading of the inscription see Frere, 1972, *ibid.,* 69-72, with further references.
12 See Niblett, R., 1986, 'Evidence for the Antonine fire at Verulamium from the Wheelers' excavations', *Herts Archaeology ,*9, 29-78; also Niblett, R., and Thompson, I., (forthcoming) *Alban's Buried Towns,* English Heritage Monograph.
13 Frere, 1972, 16.

Chapter 2

1 Morris, M. and Wainwright, A., 1995, 'Iron Age and Romano-British Settlement and Economy in the Upper Bulbourne Valley, Hertfordshire', Holgate, (ed) *Chiltern Archaeology, A Handbook for the Next Decade,* The Book Castle, 68-75.

2   Dimbleby, G.W., 1978, 'A pollen analysis from Verulamium (St Michaels 1966)', *Hertfordshire Archaeology 6*, 112-15.

3   See Part IV, 'The Environmental Evidence' in Niblett, R., 1999, *The Excavation of a Ceremonial site at Folly Lane, Verulamium,* Britannia Monograph 14, especially the sections on palynology by Wiltshire, P., 346-65, and Soil Micromorphology by Macphail, R., Cruise, G.M. and Mellalieu, S.J. 365-84.

4   Wainwright in Neal, D.S., Wardle, A. and Hunn, J., *The Excavation of an Iron Age, Roman and Medieval Settlement at Gorhambury, St Albans;* English Heritage Archaeological Report 14, 213-16.

5   Stead, I. M., 1989, 'The Earliest Burials of the Aylesford Culture', in De G. Sieveking, G., Longworth, I. M. and Wilson, K. E. (eds.) *Problems in economic and social archaeology,* 401-16, Duckworth.

6   For a discussion of late Iron Age Baldock see Burleigh, G., 1995 in Holgate (ed.) *Chiltern Archaeology, A Handbook for the Next Decade,* 110, The Book Castle.

7   For a discussion of Skeleton Green and pre-Roman Braughing generally see Partridge, C., 1981, *Skeleton Green, a late Iron Age and Romano-British settlement site,* Britannia Monograph 2.

8   Stead, I. M. and Rigby, V., 1989, *Verulamium: the King Harry Lane Site,* English Heritage Archaeological Report 12, 53.

9   Haselgrove, C., 1987, *Iron Age coinage in south-east England*, British Archaeological Reports 174, 182, 186-7.

10 Bryant, S. and Niblett, R., 1997, 'The Late Iron Age in Hertfordshire and the north Chilterns' in Gwilt, A. and Haselgrove, C. (eds), *Reconstructing Iron Age Societies*, Oxbow monograph 71, 270-81.

11 Neal, D.S., Wardle, A. and Hunn, J., 1990, *The Excavation of the Iron Age, Roman and Medieval Settlement at Gorhambury, St Albans,* English Heritage Archaeological Report 14.

12 Neal *et al., ibid.,* 14-22.

13 I am grateful to Simon West for information from his excavations in 1996.

14 Frere, 1983, *ibid.,* 5.

15 *Britannia XXV,* 1994, 276; *Britannia XXVI,* 1995, 354.

16 Haselgrove, C. and Millett, M., 1997, 'Verlamion Reconsidered', in Haselgrove and Gwilt, *ibid.,* 291; Macreth, D., 1999, 'The Brooches' in Niblett, 1999, *ibid.,* 219.

17 Niblett, R., 1999, *The Excavation of a Ceremonial site at Folly Lane, Verulamium,* Britannia Monograph 14.

18 Mays, S., 1999, 'The Human Bone', in Niblett, *ibid.,* 319.

19 Information from Simon West.

20 Roymans, N., 1996, 'The sword or the plough.   Regional dynamics in the Romanization of Belgic Gaul', in Roymans, N. (ed.), *From the Sword to the Plough',* 29-31.

21 Macphail, R. *et al.* 1999 in Niblett, *ibid.,* 381-4.

22 Caesar, *De Bello Gallico, V,* 19.

23 Neal *et al.,* 1990, *ibid.,* 208.

24 Caesar, *De Bello Gallico* V, 18.

25   Wheeler and Wheeler, 1936, *ibid.*, 19-22.

26   Partridge, 1981, *ibid.*, 323-50.

27   Stevens, C.E., 1951, 'Britain between the invasions' in Grimes, W.F. (ed.), *Aspects of Archaeology in Britain and beyond,* 232-44.

28   Strabo, IV, 5.3.

29   Creighton, J., 2000, *Coins and Power in Late Iron Age Britain,* Cambridge University Press.

Chapter 3

1   For a recent discussion of the theory see Bird, D.G., 2000, 'The Claudian Invasion Campaigns reconsidered', *The Oxford Journal of Archaeology* Vol. 19, 1, 91-104. See also Black, E.W., 2000, 'Sentius Saturninus and the Roman Invasion of Britain', *Britannia* XXXI, 1-10.

2   Tacitus, *Annales XIV,* 45.

3   Barrett, A.A., 1991, 'Claudius' British Victory Arch in Rome', *Britannia* XXII, 1-19.

4   Greep, S.J., 1987, 'Lead Sling-shots from Windridge Farm, St Albans, and the use of the Sling in the Roman Army in Britain', *Britannia* XVIII, 183-200.

5   Frere, 1983, *ibid.*, 4-5.

6   Anthony, I., 1970, 'Excavations in St Michaels, 1966', *Hertfordshire Archaeology* 2, 41-51.

7   Reece, R., 1984, 'The Roman Coins' in Frere, S.S., *Verulamium Excavations Volume 3.*

8   Niblett, R., 1993, 'Verulamium since the Wheelers' in Greep, S. (ed.), *The Wheeler Inheritance,* Council for British Archaeology Research Report no.93, 78-92.

9   Roymans, N., 1996, *ibid.,* 28-35.

10   Foster, J., 1999, 'The Funerary Finds', in Niblett, *ibid.*, 175-6.

11   Stead and Rigby, 1989, *ibid.*, 83.

12   Information from the excavator, Simon West.

13   Frere, 1983, *ibid.*, 121 (where it was interpreted as a natural feature); Anthony, I., 1961, 'Excavation of the Roman Street beneath St Michael's Bakery, Verulamium', *Trans. St Albans Architect. & Archaeol. Society,* 1961, 36-43.

14   Frere, 1972, *ibid.*, fig. 8.

15   Black, E.W., 1997, 'Flue tiles in Britannia: the Spread of Roman Bathing in the First and Second Centuries', *Archaeological Journal* 153, 60-78.

16   I am grateful to the excavator, Chris Saunders for information on this site. See also *Britannia* VI, 258 and Frere, 1983, *ibid.*, 8.

17   See for instance the Forum plans in Frere, 1983, *ibid.*, figs. 22-4.

18   Frere, 1983, *ibid.*, fig. 4; Wacher, J., 1992, *Towns in Roman Britain,* fig. 101, Batsford.

19   Millett, M., 1987, 'Boudicca, the First Colchester Potters' Shop and the dating of Neronian samian', *Britannia* XVIII, 104.

20   Saunders, C. and Havercroft, A.B., 1977, 'A kiln of the potter Oastrius and related excavations at Little Munden Farm, Bricket Wood', *Herts Archaeology* 3 109-56.

21   Wheeler and Wheeler, 1936, *ibid.*, plate CXIX.

22   For a discussion of the inscription see Frere, 1983, *ibid.*, 69-72.

23   Page, W. and Taylor, M.V., 1914, *Victoria County History of the County of Hertfordshire: vol. 4, part 5: Celtic and Romano-British remains,* 130-35.

24   Lowther, A.W.G., 1935, 'Verulamium: Insulae XII and XIII. A note on excavations during 1934 and 1935', *Trans. St Albans Architect & Archaeol. Soc.,* 312-16; Corder, P., 1940, 'Excavations in the forum of Verulamium (Insula XII) 1939', *Antiquaries Journal,* 500-3.

25   Cotton M.A. and Wheeler, R.E.M., 1953, 'Verulamium 1949', *Trans. St Albans Architect. & Archaeol. Soc.,* 13–97.

26   Ashdown, C., 1893, *St Albans historical and picturesque, with an account of the Roman city of Verulamium,* Elliot Stock.

27   Montague-Puckle, F.H.G. and Niblett, R., 1986, 'Observations on the south-east side of the Basilica', *Hertfordshire Archaeology* 9, 178-82.

28   Frere, 1972, *ibid.,* 76-7.

29   Wheeler and Wheeler, 1936, *ibid.,* 49-58.

30   Wheeler notebook 24, Verulamium Museum Archive.

31   Wheeler and Wheeler, 1936, *ibid.,* pl. xviii.

32   Hunn, J., 1992, 'The Verulamium Oppidum and its landscape,' *Archaeol. Journ.,* 149, 49.

33   I am grateful to Mr Rawlins who sent me notes and comments on his work on this ditch.

34   Wheeler and Wheeler, 1936, *ibid.,* 74, pl. XX, section C-D.

Chapter 4

1   Frere, 1983, *ibid.,* 73-98.

2   Manning, W., Niblett, R. and Saunders, C., publication forthcoming.

3   Wheeler and Wheeler, 1936, *ibid.,* 78-83.

4   Frere, 1983, *ibid.,* 237; fig. 95.

5   Wheeler and Wheeler, 1936, *ibid.,* 93-6.

6   Neal, D., Wardle, A., and Hunn, J., 1990, *Excavation of the Iron Age, Roman and Medieval Settlement at Gorhambury, St Albans,* English Heritage Archaeological Report no.14.

7   Neal, D.S., 1974, *The Excavation of the Roman Villa at Gadebridge Park, Hemel Hempstead, 1963-8,* Report of the Research Committee of the Society of Antiquaries of London, XXXI.

8   For Dicket Mead, east of Welwyn, see Rook, T., 1987, 'A Roman Villa Site at Dicket Mead, *Herts Archaeol 9*; Park Street, O'Neil, H., 1945, 'The Roman Villa at Park Street, near St Albans', *Archaeological Journal CII,* 31-110, and Saunders, A.D., 1961, 'Excavations at Park Street, 1954-7', *Archaeological Journal CXVIII,* 100-35.

9   Lowther, A.W.G., 1939, 'Report on the Excavation of the Roman Structure at Rothamsted Experimental Station, Harpenden', *St Albans and Herts Architectural & Archaeological Society Transactions,* 108-14.

10   Neal, D.S., 1984, 'A Sanctuary at Wood Lane End, Hemel Hempstead, Herts', *Britannia XIV,* 193-216.

11   Saunders, C. and Havercroft, A.B., 1977, 'A Kiln of the Potter Oastrius and Related Excavations at Little Munden Farm, Bricket Wood', *Herts Archaeology 5*, 109-56.

12   Saunders, A.D., 1961, 'Excavations at Park Street, 1954-7', *Archaeol. Journ. CXVIII,* 118.

13   Frere, 1972, *ibid.,* 76-7.

14   Locker, A., 1999, 'The Animal Bone' in Niblett, R., *The Excavation of a Ceremonial Site at Folly Lane, Verulamium*, Britannia Monograph 14, 334.

15   Information John Peter Wild.

16   The site was partially excavated by the Herts Archaeological Trust, and I am grateful to Claire Halpin for information on the site.

17   Information Stuart Bryant.

18   Wheeler and Wheeler, 1936, *ibid.,* pl. xxvii.

19   Both sites were partially excavated by the Herts Archaeological Trust in advance of pipeline construction, and I am grateful to Claire Halpin for information on them.

20   Pliny, *Natural History XIV, xviii,* 149.

21   Verulamium Museum archive; Wheeler notebook 6.

22   Fulford, M. and Timby, J., 2000, *Late Iron Age and Roman Silchester: Excavations on the site of the Forum Basilica,* Britannia Monograph 15, 76.

23   Niblett, R., 1987, 'Evidence for the Antonine Fire at Verulamium from the Wheelers excavations', *Hertfordshire Archaeology 9,* 29-78.

24   Frere, 1983, *ibid.,* 14.

25   Wheeler notebook 21, Verulamium Museum archive.

26   It was found in the bed of the river Ver where it had lain for many years. It had probably been abandoned by stone robbers attempting to remove it for reuse in the town. The massive masonry footings reported in a gas pipe trench near the point at which the Devils Dyke was crossed by Watling street might be the foundations for a monumental tomb of this sort.

27   Information from the excavator, Adrian Havercroft.

28   Wheeler and Wheeler, *ibid.,* pl. xxiv.

29   Frere, 1983, *ibid.,* 300-1, fig. 129, nos. 172-3.

30   Wheeler and Wheeler, 1936, *ibid.,* 58-63.

31   Frere, 1983, *ibid.,* 53.

32   Frere, 1983, *ibid.,* 277-81.

33   Reece, R., 1984, 'The Coins', in Frere, *ibid.,* 17.

Chapter 5

1   Wheeler and Wheeler, 1936, *ibid.,* 28.

2   Wheeler and Wheeler, 1936, *ibid.,* 31-2.

3   Collingwood, R.G. and Myres, J.L.N., 1936, *Roman Britain and the English Settlements,* 205.

4   Frere, S., 1983, *ibid.,* 16.

5   Niblett, R., 1993, 'Verulamium since the Wheelers', in Greep, S. (ed.), *Roman Towns: the Wheeler Inheritance,* Council for British Archaeology Res. Rep. 93, 90-1.

6   These were not included in the published report.

7   Frere, S., 1983, *ibid.*, 198-9.

8   Richardson, K., 1944, 'Excavations at Verulamium, Insula XVII, 1938', *Archaeologia* 90, fig. 4.

9   Frere, 1983, *ibid.*, 134, 151, 157, 250.

10 Grover, J.W., 1869, 'Verulam and Pompeii compared', *Journ. British Archaeological Association* 47.

11 Wheeler and Wheeler, 1936, *ibid.*, 32-4.

12 Frere, 1983, *ibid.*, 93-101.

13 Frere, 1983, *ibid.*, 23-5, 220.

14 White R. and Barker, P., 1998, *Wroxeter, the Rise and Fall of a Roman town*, Tempus, 118-30.

15 Lowther, A.W.G., 1937, 'Report on Excavations at Verulamium in 1934', *Antiq. Journ.* XVII, 28-55.

16 Wheeler and Wheeler, 1936, *ibid.*, 122-3, pl. xxxv.

17 Anthony, I.E., 1968, 'Excavations in Verulam Hills Field, St Albans, 1963-4', *Herts Archaeol.* 1, 9-50.

18 Constantius.*Vita Sancti Germani*. Trans. R.H. Niblett.

19 *Passio Albani* (Turin version). Trans. R.H. Niblett.

20 For a convenient summary of the arguments see Morris, J., 1968, 'The date of St Alban', *Herts Archaeol.* 1, 1-8.

21 Biddle, B. and Biddle, M., 1996, 'The quest for Alban continued: excavations south of the Abbey in 1995', *Alban Link* 45, 10-22.

22 Information from the site's excavators, Chris Saunders and Simon West.

23 Niblett, 1999, *ibid.*, fig. 44.

24 Excavated by A.B. Havercroft in 1986, Verulamium Museum archive.

25 White and Barker, 1998, *ibid.*, 118-30.

26 I am grateful to Simon West for information on this excavation.

27 Riley, H.E. (ed.), 1867, *Gesta Abbatum monasterii S. Albani, Voume 1,* Rolls Society, 121-2.

28 The whole question of Kingsbury and Saxon St Albans is discussed in Niblett, R. and Thompson I., *Albans Buried Towns,* English Heritage Monograph, forthcoming.

29 Williamson, T., 2000, *The Origins of Hertfordshire*, Manchester University press, 92.

30 Stead, I. M. and Rigby, V., 1989, *Verulamium: the King Harry Lane Site,* English Heritage Archaeological Report 12, 77-9, 225-39.

31 Bede, *Historia Ecclesiastica Gentis Anglorum,* vol. I, VII, 20, Stevenson, J. (ed.), 1838. It was these people who gave their name to Watling Street.

Further reading

General

For an up-to-date general account of Roman Britain see Peter Salway's *The Oxford Illustrated History of Roman Britain* (Oxford, 1993). Martin Millett's *The Romanisation of Roman Britain* (Cambridge University Press, 1990) and *An Atlas of Roman Britain* by Barri Jones and David Mattingly (Oxford, 1990) also provide excellent accounts of the province while Sheppard Frere's *Britannia* (Routledge, 1987) is still a standard work and includes a comprehensive survey of the history of the province. Particular aspects of Roman Britain are dealt with in more specialised works. For Romano-British towns in general see John Wacher's *Towns in Roman Britain* (Routledge, 1995, 2nd edition) and Barry Burnham and John Wacher's *Small Towns in Roman Britain* (Batsford, 1990). Both books include detailed accounts of Romano-British towns, providing a useful background against which to view the history of Verulamium. A collection of papers published in *The Roman Villa in Britain* (Routledge, 1969) was edited by A.L.F. Rivet and provides a good introduction to the subject, while *Rural Settlement in Roman Britain* by Richard Hingley (Seaby, 1989) provides a comprehensive review of the Romano-British countryside. John Wacher's *A Portrait of Roman Britain* (Sutton, 2000) gives an interesting overview of the visual aspects of the province, with particular reference to towns. The various religious cults and practices are fully discussed in *The Gods of the Celts* by Miranda Green (Gloucester, 1986) and *Religion in Roman Britain* by Martin Henig (Batsford 1984); the evidence for Christianity is examined in all its aspects in Charles Thomas' *Christianity in Roman Britain to AD 500* (Batsford, 1981). Wall paintings, mosaics, carved gemstones and fine metalwork are discussed in Martin Henig's *The Art of Roman Britain* (Batsford, 1995), while the collection of papers published in the Council for British Archaeology's Research Report 94, *Architecture in Roman Britain* (edited by Peter Johnson with Ian Hayes, 1996) also contains much useful material. Useful summaries of the later history of Roman Britain are provided by *The Ending of Roman Britain* by Simon Esmonde Cleary (Batsford, 1989) and *The Golden Age of Roman Britain* by Guy de la Bédoyère (Tempus, 1999).

Verulamium and its region

As will have become clear from the references in the text the standard works for most work in Verulamium itself are *Verulamium: a Belgic and Two Roman Cities*, by R.E.M. and T.V. Wheeler (1936) and the three volumes of *Verulamium Excavations* by Sheppard Frere which were published in 1972 (volume I), 1983 (volume II) and 1984 (volume III). These are complemented by the three volumes detailing excavations in the immediate vicinity, *Verulamium: the King Harry Lane Site'* by Ian Stead and Valery Rigby (English Heritage Archaeological Report no. 12, 1989), *The Excavation of an Iron Age, Roman and Medieval*

Settlement at Gorhambury, St Albans by D.S. Neal, J. Hunn and A. Wardle (English Heritage Archaeological Report no.14, 1990) and *A Ceremonial Site at Folly Lane, Verulamium,* by R. Niblett (Britannia Monograph no. 14, 1999). For discussions of the early history of Verulamium see 'Verlamion reconsidered' by Colin Haselgrove and Martin Millett, and 'The late Iron Age in Hertfordshire and the Chilterns' by S. Bryant and R. Niblett; both papers are included in *Reconstructing Iron Age Societies,* Oxbow Monograph 71, edited by A. Gwilt and C. Haselgrove (Oxford 1997). Several comprehensive accounts of the excavation of rural sites in the hinterland of Verulamium have also been published. For villas in the region see *The Excavation of a Roman Villa in Gadebridge Park* (Society of Antiquaries of London Research Report XXI, 1974), 'Northchurch, Boxmoor and Hemel Hempstead Station: The Excavation of three Roman Buildings in the Bulbourne Valley (in *Hertfordshire Archaeology* 4, 1977), both by D.S. Neal, and 'The Roman villa at Dicket Mead, Welwyn' by Tony Rook in *Hertfordshire Archaeology* 9 (1986). Several lower status rural sites have been excavated in recent years, some of which are now published including *Foxholes Farm: A multi-period gravel site* by Clive Partridge (Herts Archaeological Trust, 1989) and *Excavations at Boxfield Farm, Chells, Stevenage* by C.J. Going and J.R. Hunn, published by the Herts Archaeological Trust in 1999. For settlement patterns in the area at the end of the Iron Age see *Settlement patterns in south-west Herts* by J. Hunn (British Archaeological Reports no. 249, Oxford, 1996) and the first two chapters in Tom Williamson's *The Origins of Hertfordshire* (Manchester University Press, 2000). Keith Branigan's *The Catuvellauni* (Sutton, 1985) and *Roman Hertfordshire* by R. Niblett (Dovecote Press, 1995) contain general overviews of settlement in the area in the Roman period. Two major archaeological societies, the East Hertfordshire Archaeological Society and the St Albans and Hertfordshire Archaeological and Architectural Society together produce the journal *Hertfordshire Archaeology* which is published periodically and contains articles and papers on a variety of archaeological and historical subjects in the area. It also includes 'round-ups' of the results of recent excavations. A useful collection of papers, many of them relevant to Verulamium, was edited by Robin Holgate and published by the Book Castle in 1995 in *Chiltern Archaeology: a handbook for the next decade.*

The recent work on St Alban and the growth of Christianity in Verulamium is not yet fully published, but an interim account is due to be published by Martin and Birthe Biddle in *The Journal of the British Archaeological Association* in 2001, along with other papers discussing the cult of St Alban. E.A. Thompson's *St Germanus of Auxerre and the end of Roman Britain* (Cambridge University Press, 1984) discusses the question of St Germanus's visit to Verulamium in 429 and is also essential reading for anyone seriously interested in the town in the early fifth century. For an excellent introductory survey of the development of the whole area surrounding Verulamium in the early medieval period see *The Origins of Hertfordshire* by Tom Williamson (Manchester University Press 2000).

Indubitably the best way to fully appreciate the wealth and variety of the remains of Roman Verulamium is through the rich collections of excavated material contained in the Verulamium Museum. Anyone with a wish to take the subject further should visit the Museum, and the remains of the town's past that are on public view — that is the town walls, the remains of the London Gate, the hypocaust and mosaic in insula IV and the Roman theatre.

Glossary

agger	a bank, either forming a rampart in a defence system, or providing a raised base for a road.
amphora	a large ceramic jar used for storing and transporting food and drink, particularly wine, olive oil and fish sauce.
Antonine	the period between 138 and 192 when Antonius Pius and his successors, Marcus Aurelius, Lucius Verus and Commodus, were emperors.
basilica	an elongated hall, often forming the law court in a Roman Forum.
burh	a late Saxon fortified settlement.
caldarium	a hot room in a Roman bath suite, heated by hypocaust and placed close to the furnace room.
cavea	the area in the theatre used to accommodate the audience.
cella	a room in a temple housing the cult statue or shrine.
chaff-tempered ware	a type of pottery made with clay that was tempered with chopped-up chaff and grass. Usually dated in the Verulamium area to between the sixth and eighth century AD.
civitas	in the case of Roman Britain a term used to describe a tribal group.
Claudian	the period between 41 and 54 when Claudius was emperor.
emmer	an early form of wheat.
Flavian	the period between 69 and 96 when Vespasian and his sons, Titus and Domitian, were emperors.
flint-gritted ware	a type of pottery made with clay that was tempered with ground-up flint.
Forum	the central market, meeting place and business centre in a Roman town.
frigidarium	an unheated room in a Roman bath suite.
grog-tempered ware	a type of pottery made with clay that was tempered with ground-up fragments of fired pottery. Common in the area from the first century BC to the late first century AD.
hypocaust	a system for heating rooms by using hot air channels under raised floors and through flues in the walls.
insula	a block of land delimited by streets within a town.
laconicum	a hot room in a Roman bathsuite; heated by hypocaust and close to the furnace, but with a dry atmosphere.

lorica	armour for the upper body, either in the form of iron mail, or iron plates hinged together with leather straps and bronze buckles, hooks and strap ends.
macellum	a market hall with small shops or booths arranged around a central court.
mansio	a guest house to accommodate officials on government service.
Martyrium	a Christian church built on the grave of a martyr.
municipium	a chartered town.
Neronian	the period between 54 and 68 when Nero was emperor.
oppidum	a term used for extensive, late pre-Roman Iron Age settlements associated with substantial linear earthworks. They were frequently associated with trading activities and/or high-status industry such as metalworking. Settlement within them tended to be polyfocal rather than nucleated.
Pelagian heresy	a late-Roman Christian heresy that emphasised the role of free will in determining an individual's salvation.
portico	a colonnade or verandah along the side of a building.
samian	a type of pottery with a glossy red slip, sometimes highly decorated. Made in Italy, south, central and eastern Gaul between the first century BC and the mid-third century AD.
spelt	an early form of wheat.
strigil	a curved metal blade used to scrape off oil from the body in a hot room in a Roman bath suite.
tepidarium	a warm room, situated between the hot and cold rooms in a Roman bath suite.
territorium	area of land associated with a town.
villa	a Romanised residential building in the countryside.

Index